Kith and Kin

Sources for family history

Compiled by

Anne Burrows
Susan Mildred
Patricia Moore
Michael Talbot

The Libraries Board of South Australia
Adelaide 1994

2nd Edition 1994
© Libraries Board of South Australia

Typesetting : Connie Iversen
Design and layout : Peter Murdoch
Photography : Narelle Karas

Printed and bound by
Gillingham Printers Pty Ltd
153 Holbrooks Road, Underdale
Adelaide, South Australia 5032

National Library of Australia Cataloguing-in-Publication Data

Kith and kin : sources for family history.

2nd ed.
Bibliography.
Includes index.
ISBN 0 7243 0200 X.

1. Mortlock Library of South Australiana - Catalogs. 2. State
Library of South Australia - Catalogs. 3. Genealogy - Bibliography
- Catalogs. 4. Genealogy - Library resources. 5. South Australia -
Genealogy - Bibliography - Catalogs. I. Burrows, Anne, 1953- .
II. Libraries Board of South Australia.

929.39423

Cover:
William Weller and his family (c.1898).
This view shows a Victorian custom of placing photographs
of deceased relatives in family group photographs.
SSL:M:B46880

CONTENTS

ACKNOWLEDGMENTS

The compilers would like to thank all State Library staff who assisted in the preparation of this edition of *Kith and kin*, in particular Connie Iversen for keyboarding the text; Peter Murdoch for assistance with the design of the work, and for converting it into Pagemaker; Narelle Karas for the photography and also Roger Andre, Patricia Elliott, Elizabeth Ho, Barbara Holbourn, Diana Honey, Peter Jenkins, Tom Lawlor, Barbara Mayfield, Susan Paul, Daniel Planquart, Beth Robertson, Anne Sinclair, Valerie Sitters, Zaiga Sudrabs, Jennifer Tonkin and Brian Tuffin. We are indebted to the State History Centre for permission to include the list of *South Australian historical organisations*, and to Brian Samuels the compiler. We would also like to thank Christina Reardon of State Records; The South Australian Genealogy and Heraldry Society Inc., and in particular Maureen Leadbeater, for the district register details; and professional historian Dr Leith MacGillivray for her advice regarding land records.

FOREWORD

This second edition of *Kith and kin* represents a commitment by the State Library of South Australia to one of its major client groups, namely to all those men and women who, whether for personal or professional purposes, choose to embark on research and enquiry into their own or someone else's family origins.

The earlier edition of *Kith and kin* filled a market niche and was quickly sold out. Since it first appeared, we have consolidated our Family History service and the collections which support it. New materials have been published, our staff continue to develop their expertise and our public use of the service continues to grow. A recent household survey of South Australians indicated that 22.3% of people would potentially use the State Library of South Australia for tracing their family history. This represents 227,088 people, so the need for research tools such as *Kith and kin* is obvious. The State Library of South Australia is committed to providing and encouraging the use of as many 'self-help' tools as possible for our clients. This is one of them. I am confident that it will serve its purpose well.

Frances H. Awcock
Director
State Library of South Australia

FAMILY HISTORY
IN THE YEAR OF THE FAMILY

How can we best describe the value of family history? Staff here know that many people find this type of research very satisfying and fulfilling. Sometimes we pause to reflect on the fact that our family history service is contributing to a positive sense of place and identity among our users and their families. For some, lost associations are regained and for others, a valuable feeling of continuity is created. Family histories encourage gatherings, they bring people together – one only has to look at the notices in the local paper to see the number of reunions which are being held. For some of our clients, family history may mean their first learning experience since school or the first time they have ever used a library as a researcher. Quite a number of beginners have gone on to become serious researchers, moving from personal family history to a wider sphere of historical interest. Those who have become expert in family history may have competed for the State Family History Award which has fostered some very fine publications indeed. Personal achievement and stronger families can often be traced back to that tentative decision to become involved in family history.

The first South Australian Family History specialist desk was created in 1986 in the newly established Mortlock Library and the first South Australian Family History librarian position was created in 1989. Soon after, the first of a series of seminars for budding family historians was held and the first edition of *Kith and kin* was published. Since then we have appointed another specialist librarian to cover Australian and international research and we have created an integrated and comprehensive Family History Collection and service. These initiatives collectively represent a new era for family history in the State Library. Many staff contribute, whether by staffing the Family History Desk, developing or acquiring databases, or ensuring microfilm is produced and equipment working.

Cooperation with the South Australian Genealogy and Heraldry Society and other agencies has been especially important in the provision of services to family historians, whether as beginners or as more experienced researchers. Their help has greatly assisted the preparation of this publication.

In this Year of the Family we are pleased to offer a new edition of *Kith and kin*. We hope you find it both comprehensive and helpful.

Elizabeth Ho
Assistant Director
State Library of South Australia
(Library Services)

ABOUT THIS BOOK

ARRANGEMENT

This book is set out in five parts.

- Part 1 is an introduction to family history research, including a select list of publications on the topic held by the State Library of South Australia.

- Part 2 describes the State Library of South Australia Family History Collection. The various sources and indexes for South Australian family history are followed by an overview of the interstate and overseas holdings in the collection.

- Part 3 concentrates on other collections in the State Library of South Australia containing material of interest to family historians:

  > Bray Reference Library including the Map Collection
  > Mortlock Library of South Australiana with special sections on:
  >> Aboriginal people of South Australia
  >> J.D. Somerville Oral History Collection
  >> Pictorial Collection
  > Rare Books and Named Collections
  > Royal Geographical Society of Australasia (SA Branch) Inc.

- Part 4 lists resources for widening your research beyond the State Library. Included is a brief list of various other South Australian government and non-government organisations that hold records of use for family research. A list of addresses of major interstate and overseas bodies is also included.

- Part 5 provides a guide to societies and research agencies that may undertake more extensive research and a list of country and regional local history societies, compiled by staff of the State History Centre, which could suggest centres of expertise on a wide range of subjects. A full list of South Australian public libraries holding district registers of South Australian birth, death and marriage records is also included.

- A general subject index begins on page 109.

ASPECTS NOT COVERED

Kith and kin concentrates on the most popularly used sources in the State Library Family History Collection. Although there are sections on other aspects of the State Library, it does not cover in detail all the possible avenues you could explore such as:

- the archival finding aids
- the biographical indexes
- the general subject index to published materials
- the catalogues of published materials (useful for published family histories and local area histories)

Aspects not covered

- various South Australian government organisations' published serials such as:
  Education Gazette
  Government Gazette
  Parliamentary Papers

Library staff will be pleased to help with information on these and any other topics.

SOURCE SHEETS

The source sheets referred to in the text are part of a continuing series compiled by the South Australian Research and Family History Team, State Library of South Australia.

Source sheets are compiled on selected subjects originated by user demand or to mark a special event in the history of South Australia. They bring together the major references on the chosen subject, and offer an easy overview of sources held by the State Library.

Source sheets may be consulted in the State Library of South Australia and public libraries throughout South Australia. Copies of source sheets are available for the usual State Library photocopying and postal charges from the South Australian Research and Family History Team, State Library of South Australia, GPO Box 419, Adelaide 5001.

For further information about source sheets contact the Source Sheet Co-ordinator on (08) 207 7236.

PRODUCTS FOR SALE

The State Library's Image Centre has produced microform copies of a number of the South Australian family history sources mentioned in *Kith and kin*. These are for sale. Orders, or requests for further details, should be sent to:

Customer Services Officer
Image Centre
State Library of South Australia
GPO Box 419
Adelaide 5001

Telephone: (08) 207 7334
Fax: (08) 207 7274

MICUNION II, a union list of other Australian institutions holding copies of microfilm and microfiche produced by Image Services is also available for sale.

Attention is drawn to products that may be purchased as they are dealt with in the text.

PART 1
WHERE TO BEGIN

Anne Burrows   *Susan Mildred*

FAMILY HISTORY LIBRARIANS

The State Library has made important innovations in the last few years to provide a more effective and efficient service for family historians. Firstly, there was our appointment as specialist Family History Librarians.

In 1992 we brought together a large number of books, pamphlets, microforms, and now computer files, to create one self-service Family History Collection combining selected South Australian, interstate and overseas materials.

Our primary role as Family History Librarians has been to provide users of the collection with specialist advice on their specific family history research topics. As well as individual consultations, we also conduct orientation sessions for interested groups.

Another aspect of our work is to compile family history source sheets. These bring together references on a particular topic, or explain some aspect of the collection.

We are continually looking for ways to make the Family History Collection more accessible. In this new edition of *Kith and kin* we highlight the genealogical resources of the State Library of South Australia and other agencies. As well as updating the information in the first edition, we have enlarged the reading list on researching family history. Significant additions such as the photographic collections on videodisk, and the *International genealogical index* are described. There is a new section on interstate and overseas resources in the Family History Collection. The lists of other organisations holding family history sources, and South Australian historical organisations have been enlarged and updated. Finally there is a section on South Australian district registers of births, deaths and marriages detailing the local public libraries that hold them, and their coverage.

We know that *Kith and kin* will be invaluable for all family historians.

Anne Burrows & Susan Mildred

START WITH THE KNOWN

In general the most efficient method of tracing your family history is to start with the known (i.e. yourself, your parents and grandparents) and then to work back through each generation researching one person at a time, building up a pattern of family events (e.g. records of births, deaths, marriages, occupations and places of residence).

Oral history from older relatives who are still alive can provide valuable background information. Also look out for family memorabilia, such as the family Bible, photographs and diaries.

It is important to read widely to get an idea of the social setting in which your ancestors lived.

Make systematic notes of the results of your research and the sources you used. This will save you wasting time and effort.

A select list of publications on researching family history, held in the State Library of South Australia, begins on page 6.

You might also consider joining your local genealogical society. Such groups are often a valuable source of advice, especially for beginners.

IF YOU PUBLISH

SOURCE ALL REFERENCES

If you publish a family history, remember to give specific references for all sources used, including newspaper articles and photographs.

If you are using material obtained from the Mortlock Library, we prefer the following location symbol to be used as acknowledgement: SSL:M.

A select list of items useful for those writing and publishing their family history is found in Family History Source Sheet No. 2. *Writing and publishing a family history.*

COPYRIGHT

Copyright protects the original expression of ideas found in a broad range of material, such as works of art, literature and music. The *Copyright Act 1968* is an Australian Federal statute that sets out what is protected by copyright, and what that protection involves.

Several publications explaining copyright are available at the State Library reference desks for consultation.

Further advice is available from the Australian Copyright Council, Suite 3, 245 Chalmers Street, Redfern 2016. Telephone (02) 318 1788.

LEGAL DEPOSIT

The Mortlock Library acquires published materials through the provisions of the *Libraries Act 1982* which requires every publisher in South Australia to deposit a copy of their publication(s) with the library for preservation. Published family histories, whether privately produced booklets or commercially printed books, are covered by this legal deposit provision.

If you are planning to publish a family history after completing your research and require clarification of the legal deposit requirements, the leaflet *Legal deposit in Australia* is available from the Mortlock Library.

Legal deposit legislation has recently been amended to ensure deposit of audiovisual items, computer disks, sound recordings or any information item produced and made publicly available in South Australia.

FAMILY HISTORY AWARD

This annual award is made by the South Australian Genealogy and Heraldry Society Inc. to the person or persons producing, in the opinion of the society, the best family history published in that calendar year by a South Australian or of a substantially South Australian family. Written applications and entries should be sent to the 'South Australian Family History Award', c/- South Australian Genealogy and Heraldry Society Inc., GPO Box 592, Adelaide 5001 (see pages 77-78). Entries must be lodged by 31 January in the year following publication.

RESEARCHING FAMILY HISTORY

A select list of publications held in the State Library of South Australia.

GENERAL

Cole, Jean A. *Tracing your family history: a general handbook.* 3rd ed. Huntingdon : Family Tree Publications, 1988.

Fitzhugh, Terrick. *The dictionary of genealogy.* 3rd ed. London : Black, 1991.

Friar, Stephen. *Heraldry for the local historian and genealogist.* Stroud, Gloucestershire; Wolfeboro Falls, NH : Allan Sutton, 1992.

Frost, Lenore. *Dating family photos 1850-1920.* Essendon, Vic. : L. Frost, c1991.

Genealogical research directory. Sydney : Library of Australian History, 1981–.

National Library of Australia. *Genealogy and heraldry in the National Library of Australia: a select guide and bibliography.* Canberra : National Library of Australia, 1988.

Robertson, Beth M. *Oral history handbook.* 3rd ed. [Adelaide] : Oral History Association of Australia (South Australian Branch), 1994.

Sheehan, Colin Gordon. *The Australian Joint Copying Project for family historians.* Brisbane : Library Board of Queensland, 1989.

SOUTH AUSTRALIA

Ancestors in archives: a guide to family history sources in the official records of South Australia. 2nd ed. North Adelaide, S. Aust. : State Records, Research and Access Services, 1994.

Button, Pat. *A free passage to paradise?: passenger lists of United Kingdom emigrants who applied for free passage to South Australia 1836-1840.* Adelaide : South Australian Genealogy and Heraldry Society, c1992.

Manning, Geoffrey H. *Manning's place names of South Australia.* [Adelaide] : G.H. Manning, 1990.

Parsons, Ronald. *Migrant ships for South Australia, 1836-1860.* Gumeracha, S. Aust. : Gould Books, 1988.

Peake, Andrew G. *The history and records of West Terrace Cemetery, Adelaide.* 2nd ed. Dulwich, S. Aust. : Tudor Australia Press, 1991.

Peake, Andrew G. *Inscriptions from West Terrace Cemetery, Adelaide.* Vol. 1 Catholic and Society of Friends Section; Vol. 2 Jewish and other sections. Limited edition. [Adelaide] : A.G. Peake, 1982–.

Peake, Andrew G. *Sources for South Australian family history.* [Adelaide] : A.G. Peake and the South Australian Genealogy and Heraldry Society, 1977.

Peake, Andrew G. *Sources for South Australian history.* Dulwich, S. Aust. : Tudor Australia Press, 1987.

Places of burial in South Australia: a cemetery transcription index. Compiled by the South Australian Genealogy and Heraldry Society. Adelaide : The Society, 1989.

Sexton, Robert Thomas. *Shipping arrivals and departures: South Australia 1627-1850: a guide for genealogists and maritime historians.* [Ridgehaven, S. Aust.] : Gould Books, c1990.

Statton, Jill. *Burial orders 1926-1944.* Gumeracha, S. Aust. : Gould Books in association with Branch-Out Research and Services, 1989.

Statton, Jill. *Burial orders 1945-1954.* Gumeracha, S. Aust. : Gould Books in association with Branch-Out Research and Services, 1990.

Statton, Jill. *Coroner's reports 1879-1899.* Gumeracha, S. Aust. : Gould Books in association with Branch-Out Research and Services, 1988.

Statton, Jill. *Coroner's reports 1900-1910.* Gumeracha, S. Aust. : Gould Books in association with Branch-Out Research and Services, 1988.

Statton, Jill. *Deaths in public institutions.* Gumeracha, S. Aust. : Gould Books in association with Branch-Out Research and Services, 1989. (Comprises deaths of inmates of Glenside Hospital, Adelaide Asylum and Magill Home, from 1879-1951.)

Statton, Jill. *Inquests 1880-1942.* Gumeracha, S. Aust. : Gould Books in association with Branch-Out Research and Services, 1988.

Statton, Jill. *Mental patients' estates.* Gumeracha, S. Aust. : Gould Books in association with Branch-Out Research and Services, 1990.

Whitworth, Robert P. *Bailliere's South Australian gazetteer and road guide: containing the most recent and accurate information as to every place in the colony.* Adelaide : F.F. Bailliere, 1866. Facsimile: Ridgehaven, S. Aust. : Gould Books, 1991.

SOUTH AUSTRALIA – BIOGRAPHY

Biographical index of South Australians 1836-1885. Editor Jill Statton. Marden, S. Aust. : South Australian Genealogy and Heraldry Society, 1986. 4v.

Cockburn, Stewart. *The patriarchs.* Adelaide : Ferguson Publications, 1983.

Coxon, Howard et al. *Biographical register of the South Australian Parliament 1857-1957.* Netley, S. Aust. : Wakefield Press, c1985.

Crowley, F.K. *South Australian history: a survey for research students.* Adelaide : Libraries Board of South Australia, 1966. (Chapter 7 – Biography.)

Cumming, Denis Arthur and Moxham, G.A. *They built South Australia: engineers, technicians, manufacturers, contractors and their work.* [Adelaide] : D.A. Cumming and G.A. Moxham, 1986.

The Cyclopedia of South Australia in two volumes : an historical and commercial review, descriptive and biographical, facts, figures, and illustrations: an epitome of progress. Edited by Henry T. Burgess. Adelaide : Cyclopedia Co., 1907-1909. 2v.

Hardacre, Stephen. *Made in Adelaide: the people.* Photography [by] Stephen Hardacre, Denys Finney; written by Marie Appleton, including the Satchell tapes. Adelaide : Savvas Publishing, 1987.

Hoad, J. L. *Hotels and publicans in South Australia 1836-1984.* Adelaide : Australian Hotels Association (South Australian Branch) : Gould Books, 1986.

Let's not forget: obituaries of the Burra district and environs 1848-1976. Compiled by members of the Burra Community Library. Burra, S. Aust. : Burra Community Library Board of Management, 1987.

Loyau, George E. *Notable South Australians, or colonists – past and present.* Adelaide : Carey, Page & Co., 1885.

Loyau, George E. *The representative men of South Australia.* Adelaide : Howell, 1883.

Morrison, W. Frederic. *The Aldine history of South Australia, illustrated: embracing sketches and portraits of her noted people...* Sydney : Aldine Publishing Co., 1890.

Peake, Andrew G. *Sources for South Australian biography.* 2nd ed. [Dulwich, S. Aust.] : A.G. Peake, 1983, c1982.

Register personal notices. Edited by Reg Butler and Alan Phillips. Gumeracha, S. Aust. : Gould Books, c1989–. 3v.

Ross, Graham R. *Alberton Cemetery: ... computer printouts of Alberton Cemetery records.* [Port Adelaide, S. Aust. : G.R. Ross, 1990?] (Burials 1846-1930; lessees 1852-1874; burials not in registers 1869-1905; possible burials 1870-1881; tombstones.)

South Australians 1836-1885. Edited by Jan Thomas. Adelaide : South Australian Genealogy and Heraldry Society Inc., 1990. 2v.

AUSTRALASIA

Australian Archives. *Relations in records: a guide to family history sources in the Australian Archives.* Canberra : AGPS Press, 1988.

Nicholson, Ian Hawkins. *Log of logs: a catalogue of logs, journals, shipboard diaries, letters and all forms of voyage narratives, 1788 to 1988, for Australia and New Zealand, and surrounding oceans.* Aranda, ACT : Roebuck, [1990].

Nicholson, Ian Hawkins. *Log of logs. Volume two: a catalogue of logs, journals, shipboard diaries, letters and all forms of voyage narratives, 1788 to 1993 for Australian and New Zealand and surrounding oceans.* Yaroomba, Qld : I.H. Nicholson, 1993.

Peake, Andrew G. *Bibliography of Australian family history.* Dulwich, S. Aust. : Tudor Australia Press, 1988.

Peake, Andrew G. *National register of shipping arrivals: Australia and New Zealand.* 3rd ed. Sydney : Australasian Federation of Family History Organisations, 1992.

Resources for Aboriginal family history. Edited by Rodney Lucas. Canberra : Australian Institute of Aboriginal Studies, 1986.

Sexton, Rae. *The deserters: a complete record of military and naval deserters in Australia and New Zealand, 1800-65.* Rev. ed. Magill, S. Aust. : Australasian Maritime Historical Society, 1985.

Smith, Diane and Halstead, Boronia. *Lookin for your mob: a guide to tracing Aboriginal family trees.* Canberra : Aboriginal Studies Press, 1990.

Vine Hall, N. J. *Parish registers in Australia: a list of originals, transcripts, microforms and indexes of Australian parish registers.* 2nd ed. Middle Park, Vic. : N. Vine Hall, c1990.

Vine Hall, N. J. *Tracing your family history in Australia: a guide to sources.* Adelaide : Rigby, 1985.

The War dead of the Commonwealth: the register of the names of those who fell in the 1939-1945 War and are buried in cemeteries in Australia: cemeteries in South Australia and in Northern Territory. Compiled and published by order of the Commonwealth War Graves Commission. London : The Commission, 1962.

OTHER STATES

Archives Authority of New South Wales. *An introduction to sources for genealogical research.* Sydney : Archives Authority of New South Wales, 1990.

Baker, Wendy and McBeth, Sue. *Family and local history indexes in Victoria.* Hampton, Vic. : Macbeth Genealogical Books, 1988.

The Bicentennial dictionary of Western Australians, pre-1829-1888. Nedlands, WA. : University of Western Australia, 1987–.

Family and local history sources in Victoria. Edited by Frances Brown et al. 5th ed. Blackburn, Vic. : Custodians of Records, 1992.

Harrison, Jennifer. *The Archives Office of New South Wales genealogical research kit.* Brisbane : Library Board of Queensland, 1989.

J.S. Battye Library of Western Australian History. *Tracing your ancestors: a guide to genealogical sources in the J.S. Battye Library of Western Australian history.* Perth : Library Board of WA, 1983.

Local and family history sources in Tasmania. Edited by Anne M. Bartlett. Launceston, Tas. : Genealogical Society of Tasmania, 1991.

McCorkindale, Shirley. *Unlocking the past: guide to family history and genealogical resources in the State Library of Queensland.* Brisbane : Library Board of Queensland, 1988.

McIntyre, Perry. *The Queensland source book: a guide to the repositories and resources available to the local and family historian in Queensland, Australia.* Blackwater, Qld : P. McIntyre, c1986.

Northern Territory dictionary of biography. Edited by David Carment et al. Casuarina, NT : NTU Press, 1990–.

West, Linda. *Sources of information in the State Library of NSW collection on births, deaths and marriages in New South Wales.* Sydney : State Library of New South Wales, c1987.

Whitton, K. and Whitton, A. *Whitton's index to the Mercury.* Hobart : GST Inc., Hobart Branch, 1993.

Young, Faye and Harris, Don. *Birth, death and marriage certificates in Australia.* Oakleigh, Vic. : Australian Institute of Genealogical Studies, [1985], c1983.

OVERSEAS

Baxter, Angas. *Tracing your origins: a complete guide to discovering your English, Welsh, Scottish and Irish ancestors.* North Ryde, NSW : Methuen Australia, 1983, c1982.

Baxter, Angas. *In search of your European roots: a complete guide to tracing your ancestors in every country in Europe.* Baltimore, MD : Genealogical Publishing Co., 1985.

Chorzempa, Rosemary A. *Polish roots = Korzenie polski.* Baltimore, MD : Genealogical Publishing, 1993.

Cole, Jean A. *Tracing your family history: a general handbook.* 3rd ed. Huntingdon: Family Tree Publications, 1988.

Jensen, L.O. *A genealogical handbook of German research.* Pleasant Grove, Utah : L.O. Jensen, 1980-c1983.

Pedersen, Sue. *Searching overseas: a guide to family history sources for Australians and New Zealanders.* 2nd ed. Kenthurst, NSW : Kangaroo Press, 1989.

Preece, F.S. and Preece, P.P. *Handy guide to Italian genealogical records.* Logan, Utah : Everton Publishers, c1978.

Saul, Pauline A. and Markwell, F.C. *The family historian's enquire within.* 4th ed. Newbury, Berkshire : Countryside Books in association with the Federation of Family History Societies, 1991.

Schenk, Trudy et al. *The Wuerttemberg emigration index.* Salt Lake City, Utah : Ancestry Inc., 1986–. 5v.

Suess, Jared H. *Handy guide to Hungarian genealogical records.* Logan, Utah : Everton Publishers, c1980.

Suess, Jared H. *Handy guide to Swiss genealogical records.* Logan, Utah : Everton Publishers, 1978.

Wagner, Anthony. *English genealogy.* 3rd ed. Chichester, Sussex : Phillimore, 1983.

WRITING AND PUBLISHING

Beaumont, Joanna. *How to write and publish your family history: a complete guide for Australia and New Zealand.* Sydney : Orlando Press, 1985.

Brown, Frances et al. *Family and local history: an ordered approach towards publication.* Blackburn, Vic. : Custodians of Records, 1988.

Gray, Nancy. *Compiling your family history: a guide to procedures.* 19th ed. Sydney : Published jointly by ABC Enterprises and the Society of Australian Genealogists for the Australian Broadcasting Corporation, 1993.

Meadley, Dom. *Writing a family history.* 2nd ed. Nunawading, Vic. : Meadley Family History Services, 1990.

Phillips, Alan. *Desktop publishing for family historians: a brief introduction and guide.* 2nd ed. Gumeracha, S. Aust. : Gould Books, 1990.

Worthington, Janet R. *Computers for genealogy: a guide.* 5th ed. Lane Cove, NSW : Worthington Clark Pty Ltd, 1992.

PART 2
STATE LIBRARY OF SOUTH AUSTRALIA
FAMILY HISTORY COLLECTION

Researchers using material from the State Library Family History Collection in the main chamber of the Mortlock Library (March 1994).

INTRODUCTION

The Family History Collection is housed in the Jervois Wing of the State Library.

Location:	Jervois Wing State Library of South Australia North Terrace Adelaide 5000
Postal Address:	GPO Box 419 Adelaide 5001
Telephone:	Enquiries (08) 207 7360 SA Country callers 008 182 013
Hours:	Monday to Friday 9.30 am to 8.00 pm Saturday, Sunday 12.00 pm to 5.00 pm Closed on public holidays

This self-service collection on open access was established in April 1992 and was formed by the amalgamation of two already existing self-service collections of family history material – South Australian from the Mortlock Library of South Australiana and material with an interstate/overseas focus from the Bray Reference Library. It contains a number of records from the former South Australian Archives, including copies of some South Australian government records. Government records are not usually held by the State Library.

Owing to space constraints, the State Library Family History Collection is relatively small. Excluded from the collection are South Australian preservation and original items, and published family histories which are held in the Mortlock Library of South Australiana described more fully in Part 3. Family historians will also find many useful resources in the collections of the Bray Reference Library (see pages 49-50).

SERVICES AVAILABLE

State Library staff are pleased to advise family historians on possible sources of information and appropriate finding aids. They can also help you to use the various sources and indexes. For those requiring further advice a Family History Librarian may be consulted by arrangement.

While our staff assist people as much as possible, we are unable to conduct extensive family history research. For other agencies that will undertake research for a fee, see Part 5 of this guide (page 91).

SEMINARS

Introductory seminars on the resources available in the Family History Collection are held regularly. Telephone the Family History Librarians on (08) 207 7235 if you would like your name included on the mailing list.

SOUTH AUSTRALIAN SOURCES

The following topics are covered in this section:

> Adoption and fostering of children in South Australia
> Applications for assisted passage
> Biographical tools
> Births, deaths and marriages
> Census
> Directories
> Electoral rolls
> Naturalization
> Newspaper sources
> Papers relative to South Australia
> Portraits
> Shipping and passenger lists:
> > introduction
> > arrivals
> > departures
> > general shipping sources
> > shipping photographs

Many of the early colonial records are incomplete.

The collection contains copies of some surviving colonial government records. The original records are held by State Records (see pages 80-81).

Using these sources can be frustrating at times, as we do not hold the inter-related government records.

It should be remembered that South Australia was not a convict colony. If you require further information about this aspect of South Australian history, a useful reference is chapter XII, 'The convict in South Australia' in Douglas Pike. *Paradise of dissent: South Australia 1829-1857*. Melbourne : Melbourne University Press, 1967.

ADOPTION AND FOSTERING OF CHILDREN
IN SOUTH AUSTRALIA

This is a select list of publications that provide information about adoption and fostering of children in South Australia. They are all held in the State Library Family History Collection. The *Adoption Act, 1988* was changed to give adopted people and birth-parents the rights to obtain or deny identifying information. A list of organisations that may provide assistance is also included.

PUBLICATIONS

- Dunn, Pastor D.R. 'Adoption records in Australia' in *International Congress on Family History (1st: 1988: Sydney, NSW.) A selection of papers, first International Congress on Family History and fifth Australasian Congress on Genealogy and Heraldry, Sydney, October 1988.* [Blackburn, Vic.] : Australasian Federation of Family History Organisations & Society of Australian Genealogists, 1988, pages 105-114.

- Peake, Andrew. *Sources for South Australian history.* Dulwich, SA : Tudor Australia Press, 1987. See pages 14, 30-32, 227. [Page 227 provides a brief overview of adoption as well as 'adopting out' or fostering by the (former) State Children's Department.]

- Reakes, Janet. *How to trace your missing ancestors whether living, dead or adopted.* Sydney : Hale and Iremonger, 1986.

- *Ancestors in archives: a guide to family history sources in the official records of South Australia.* 2nd ed. Adelaide : State Records, Research and Access Services, 1994. [See pages 24-30 for a list of records held that provide information on children boarded out, foster mothers, destitution, state wards, lying-in homes, etc.]

- Vine Hall, N. J. *Tracing your family history in Australia: a guide to sources.* Adelaide : Rigby, 1985. [See page 201.]

OTHER ORGANISATIONS THAT MAY ASSIST:

Government

Family Information Service
Department for Family & Community Services
4 Rowells Road
Lockleys 5032
Telephone: (08) 354 0300

State Records (See pages 80-81)
Norwich Centre
55 King William Road
North Adelaide 5006
Telephone: (08) 267 8230

Non-Government

Jigsaw SA Inc.
PO Box 567
Prospect East 5083
Telephone: (08) 344 7529

ARMS (Australian Relinquishing Mothers SA Inc.)
51 North Terrace
Hackney 5069
Telephone: (08) 362 2418 [This organisation exists in most states to provide support specifically for relinquishing mothers.]

APPLICATIONS FOR ASSISTED PASSAGE

- *Register of emigrant labourers applying for a free passage to South Australia, 1836-1841.* The Register is arranged by application number. It is available on microfilm (AJCP reels 874 and 875) and in a volume. There is an index volume to the Register which is arranged alphabetically by name. This gives the relevant entry (i.e. application) numbers. In some cases, an embarkation number is given. The State Library does not hold any complementary records that may have provided further information from the embarkation number.

- *Index to Register of emigrant labourers applying for a free passage to South Australia, 1836-1841.* Compiled by Douglas Pike from records held in the Public Record Office, London. (Reference number: 1529). 62v. + m/film, 9 reels + m/fiche. [commonly known as Pike's Index]. (m/fiche available for purchase : see page viii)
  This index is arranged alphabetically by name of applicant and gives age, occupation and UK address of applicant. It also records sex and age, but not the names of dependents accompanying the applicant. It does not indicate whether the applicant actually embarked or arrived in South Australia. The index was compiled outside the State Library. It is believed to be lacking a small number of entries. Where the index entry is in doubt, the Register itself may be consulted.

- Button, Pat. *A free passage to paradise? Passenger lists of United Kingdom emigrants who applied for free passage to South Australia 1836-1840.* Adelaide : SAGHS, c1992. Using the sources Pike's Index and the Register itself, as described above, Pat Button established a correlation between blocks of embarkation numbers and the particular ships to which such numbers were assigned. She also established that embarkation numbers were assigned in a rough alphabetical sequence for each vessel. Section 1 of her book consists of a 67 page listing in alphabetical order of all applicants who were allocated embarkation numbers, together with the ship and the ship's date of arrival in South Australia.

BIOGRAPHICAL TOOLS

The Mortlock Library of South Australiana (see pages 53-54) has card indexes that cover mainly early colonists and prominent South Australians. Most of the references are to information in published sources.

- South Australiana Source Sheet no. 3. *South Australian biography* lists major published biographical sources.

Two important publications are:

- *Biographical index of South Australians, 1836-1885.* Editor Jill Statton. Marden, S. Aust.: South Australian Genealogy and Heraldry Society, 1986. 4v
  The volumes are arranged alphabetically by name of people who lived in South Australia during the period 1836-1885. Biographical details may include parents' names, birth and death dates, date of arrival in South Australia, occupation, place of residence, religion and marriage details. There is a cross-reference listing in volume IV that links former or maiden surnames of spouse to the entry surname.

- *South Australians, 1836-1885.* Edited by Jan Thomas. Adelaide : South Australian Genealogy and Heraldry Society, 1990. 2v.
  These two volumes contain new biographical entries and updates for some previous entries published in the *Biographical index of South Australians.* They replace the *Bicentennial bulletins 1-8* with additional information added to a significant number of the original entries. Each entry lists the sources from which the data were obtained. A list of contributors is included in the volumes.

Published family histories and local histories contain valuable biographical information. While there are some published lists and bibliographies available, the State Library catalogues provide the most comprehensive and up-to-date record of these publications.

BIRTHS, DEATHS AND MARRIAGES

INTRODUCTION

From 1 July 1842, all South Australian births, deaths and marriages were required to be registered. For various reasons, some were not recorded or were incorrectly recorded. Before this date various sources, including church records, provide unofficial evidence for births, deaths and marriages.

This section is arranged as follows:

- Baptisms, burials and marriages prior to official records.
- Indexes to official records (after 1 July 1842).
- Newspaper sources.
- Deaths on board emigrant ships.
- Additional sources of information.

BAPTISMS, BURIALS & MARRIAGES PRIOR TO OFFICIAL RECORDS

Church registers provide most records before the commencement of civil registration.

Baptisms before 1 July 1842

- *Baptisms at Holy Trinity Church. Dec. 1836-1843.* (Reference: Trinity Church Register of Baptisms from SRG 94/2/2). 1v.
  Details given are date; child's given name; father's surname, given name and profession; mother's given name; and name of person who performed the ceremony.

  Index: There is an alphabetical name index arranged in two parts; the first part is to children and the second part to parents. The page reference to the Trinity Church Register of Baptisms is given for each person. 1v.
  Note: Baptisms often took place months and even years after the birth occurred.

Reduced extract from the baptismal register of 1869 of Holy Trinity Church, Adelaide (SRG 94/2/2).

Burials before 1 July 1842

- *Record of deaths. Feb. 1802-Aug. 1842.* (Reference number: 1485. Original at State Records. GRG 56/68/20). 1v. + m/film, 1 reel.
  This material was compiled from the Holy Trinity Church burial register, the West Terrace burial register and selected printed sources recording deaths. It includes abstracts of sources. Details given are name, place of residence, burial date (death date is seldom recorded) and age. Cause of death is rarely given. There is a name index on pages 121-138.

Marriages before 1 July 1842

- *Record of marriages. Sept. 1836-1842.* (Reference number: 1486. Original at State Records. GRG 56/68/21). 1v. + m/film, 1 reel. [includes Roman Catholic marriages to March 1844].
  Compiled from church registers and South Australian newspapers, the material includes abstracts of sources. Details provided are name, date, place of marriage, celebrant and place of residence. There is a name index on pages 72-80.

- *Index to marriages. 1836-July 1842.* (Reference number: 1290. Original at State Records. GRG 56/68/18). 1v. + m/film, 1 reel.
  This material was compiled from church registers, South Australian newspapers and archival sources. The index is arranged alphabetically by name and gives the date of marriage and where the marriage is recorded.

- *Holy Trinity Church, Adelaide. Lists of entries in the marriage register prior to compulsory registration. July 1836-June 1842.* (Reference number: 1252). 1v.
  Details given are number of entry, name of parties, and in most cases, where they came from. Some entries also have a red number appearing by the names. These entries have notes to them which appear after page 32 . Following the notes is an index which is arranged alphabetically by name and gives the entry number for each name.

INDEXES TO OFFICIAL RECORDS (AFTER 1 JULY 1842)

The State Library holds only the microfiche indexes to official South Australian birth, death and marriage records and **not** the actual records.

If the official details of a particular person's birth, death or marriage are required, it is necessary to apply in writing or visit the Births, Deaths and Marriages Principal Registry Office (see page 71). It will be necessary to complete an application form and pay the appropriate fee to obtain a copy of the record.

A second set of registers was maintained for varying dates by district registry offices. Following the closure of the district registry offices these registers have recently been lodged with relevant local public libraries where they may be consulted but not photocopied (see pages 102-108).

Family History Collection Holdings

- *Index to birth, death and marriage records held by the Births, Deaths and Marriages Principal Registry Office. July 1842-1916.* m/fiche.

  The indexes are arranged alphabetically by name within specific periods.

  Births: 1842-67*; 1868-77*; 1878-96; 1897-1906

  Deaths: 1842-62; 1863-77; 1878-95; 1896-1905; 1906-15

  Marriages: 1842-67; 1868-78; 1879-86; 1887-96; 1897-1906; 1907-16

  Specific dates appear in the births indexes for asterisked (*) time periods. All other references are only to book and page numbers of certificates held by the Births, Deaths and Marriages Principal Registry Office. A key to the indexes giving the year covered by the particular books is available.

- *The SURS Revision indexes to South Australian birth, death and marriage records. 1842-1906.* m/fiche. (m/fiche available for purchase : see page viii)

  Some years ago, as part of the State Unemployment Relief Scheme (SURS), additional indexes to South Australian birth, death and marriage records were created. The main value of the SURS revision index is that it includes full given names and dates of events. The indexes are arranged alphabetically by name and cover the following periods:

Births	1878-1906
Deaths	1842-1905
Marriages	1842-1906*

  *Although the marriages index states that entries cover the period to 1906, there are very few entries after 1889. The Principal Registry Office advises that not all information in the SURS revision index is accurate.

- *Cross referenced marriage records: South Australian marriages 1842-1867; 1868-1878; 1879-1886; 1887-1896; 1897-1906, 1907-1916.*
  The official marriage indexes are by single name only and give no indication of marriage partner. Thus if Jane Smith married John Jones there would be index entries under each name referring to a certificate number – but, without obtaining a copy of the certificate, there is no information that will allow those knowing one name only to find the name of the other marriage partner. Ruth Hooper and David Prime have transcribed and cross referenced the Registrar's indexes of marriages. Using the book and folio number for one of the partners (obtained from the marriage indexes described previously) this tool will in most cases provide the reference to the other partner.

ADDITIONAL SOURCES OF INFORMATION

Deaths on Board Emigrant Ships

* *List showing deaths occurring on board emigrant ships 1849-1867.* (Reference: Deaths on board emigrant ships). 1v.
  The list for the period 1849 to 5 June 1865 was taken from the *South Australian Government Gazette* of 25 January 1866, pages 75-96. There is an index to this list arranged alphabetically by name giving the *Gazette* page reference. The remainder of the list was compiled separately and there is no separate name index to it.

* Deaths also appear on some passenger lists (see *Official passenger lists mainly of immigrants arriving in South Australia under United Kingdom assisted passage schemes. 1847-1886.* (Reference number: 313) on page 34).

Church Records

A number of church records are held in the archival collections of the Mortlock Library of South Australiana (see pages 53-54).

* Anglican (Church of England)   SRG 94
* South Australian Baptist Union   SRG 465
* Congregational   SRG 95
* Methodist   SRG 4
* Presbyterian   SRG 123
* Uniting   SRG 198

Series lists for these Society Record Groups give details of specific records and their reference numbers. For some churches of these denominations, the library holds baptismal, marriage and burial registers for various periods, many of which have been microfilmed.

CENSUS

The 1841 census compiled by the Colonial Secretary's Office was the earliest South Australian census taken and is the only original census material to survive. All subsequent census returns were destroyed after statistics had been collated. In South Australia, the 1841 census is therefore unique in recording personal names. Several sources use the 1841 census or provide supplementary information to it.

- *Census returns 1841.* (Reference number: 407. Original at State Records GRG 24/13). 1v. + m/film, 1 reel + m/fiche. (m/fiche available for purchase : see page viii)
  Returns give name, age-group and locality of residence of head of household, and sex, age-group and in some cases names of others in household. Place of residence, if outside Adelaide, is usually shown as District A (surrounding Adelaide), B (South of Glenelg) or C (South of the Onkaparinga River to beyond Aldinga and Willunga).

  Index: The index to the census is arranged alphabetically by name and gives reference to the page where the name appears. 1v. (m/fiche available for purchase : see page viii)

- Arrowsmith, John. *Map showing the Special Surveys in South Australia to the Eastward of the Gulf of St. Vincent from documents in the Survey Office Adelaide.* London : John Arrowsmith, 1 March 1841. This map shows the boundaries of the various districts referred to in the 1841 census. It is held in the Map Collection (see pages 51-52).

- *Papers relative to South Australia* (see page 29). Once a reference has been found to a person residing in Districts A, B, C, etc. listed in the 1841 census, it might be worthwhile to check the *Papers relative to South Australia* for any further references to that person. *Papers relative to South Australia* are indexed in *Colonial residents of South Australia 1839-1848* (see page 23).

- Ross, Graham R. *1841 census: District of Albert Town.* [Port Adelaide, S. Aust. : G.R. Ross, 1991] is a study of a specific area using the census information.

Data collected in Albert Town, District A, for the 1841 Census. Albert Town, near Port Adelaide, later became known as Alberton. Photograph courtesy of State Records.

DIRECTORIES

DIRECTORIES AND ALMANACS

Directories are a useful source of information about people. South Australian directories on public access in the Family History Collection are listed below, together with a number of indexes and works based on them.

- *South Australian almanacks and directories, 1839-1973.*
  Microfiche: 1839-1936 (m/fiche available for purchase : see page viii)
  Volumes: 1867-1973 [1973 was the last published]
  These directories are a guide to where and for how long somebody resided in a particular place. Usually only the head of the household, generally male, was listed. No details apart from name, address and occupation are given.
  Arrangement of the directories varies over the years and this should be borne in mind before searching. From the early 1870s the directories are arranged in one alphabetical name sequence for the state, although there may also be separate country township sections and street sections for the Adelaide metropolitan area. There are also mercantile, society, ecclesiastical, legal, government and municipal listings.

- *Colonial residents of South Australia 1839-1848.* m/fiche. (m/fiche available for purchase : see page viii)
  A consolidated index on microfiche to name entries in the first ten years of the *South Australian almanacks and directories (1839-1848)* and *Papers relative to South Australia (1840)*. Each entry shows all of the information given in the particular almanac in which the name appears.

- *Index to miscellaneous information and advertisements contained in South Australian almanacks and directories 1839 to 1872.* Compiled by M. Penelope Mayo, 1947. 192 pages. formerly Acc. 1382 (Original at State Records GRG 56/68/19).
  A list of almanacs and directories indexed appears at the front, together with an explanation of symbols used. Arrangement is alphabetical by subject [i.e. personal names, places, business names, organisation names, etc.]. Cross references are also given. Primarily references are to advertisements, but headings like CIVIL SERVICE, NAME LISTS, PRICES and PUBLIC HOLIDAYS also provide information.

- *Directory of residents of Port Adelaide district – Port Adelaide, Alberton, Queenstown, Peninsula and Portland Estate (from South Australian almanacs and directories 1841-1868).* Compiled by Graham R. Ross. Port Adelaide, S. Aust. : G.R. Ross, 1989.

TELEPHONE DIRECTORIES

Telephone directories complement the directories and almanacs. They provide a useful guide to where, and for how long, a telephone service subscriber lived in a particular place. Arrangement varies over the years, but generally metropolitan and country listings exist and may need to be consulted. There are also the pink and later yellow pages – for business and service listings these are usually more accurate than the South Australian almanacs and directories. For convenience the various publicly available sets in the State Library are described here.

TELEPHONE DIRECTORIES

1898, 1913/14 – to date

- A preservation set of South Australian telephone directories covering these dates is available in the Mortlock Library of South Australiana, on request from the desk staff. As the material is for preservation, use of the other sets is encouraged wherever possible.

1933-1969 (incomplete)

- A use set of South Australian telephone directories covering this period is available on open access in the Mortlock Library.

1970-1991

- A microfiche set of South Australian telephone directories covering this period is available in the Family History Collection.

1991 – to date

- A use set of South Australian telephone directories covering this period is available on open access in the Mortlock Library.

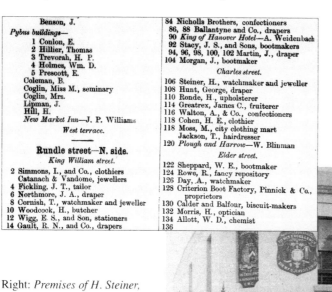

Right: *Premises of H. Steiner, Watchmaker and Jeweller of Rundle Street, Adelaide (c.1877-84). SSL:M:B10834*

Above: *Street entry published in the* Adelaide almanac and directory for South Australia *(1880).*

ELECTORAL ROLLS

Electoral rolls give the full name, address and (until recently) occupation of those people entitled to vote. The arrangement in most South Australian electoral rolls is by electoral district and then alphabetically by name. After 1987 the arrangement became a single alphabetical sequence, by name, for the whole state.

Not all electoral rolls have survived. Prior to 1987, electoral records only exist for the years in which elections were held. In South Australia, women did not have the vote until 1894.

Indexes to polling places have been published and these should be consulted to determine in what electorate a particular town or suburb appeared at a given date. It is important to remember that electoral boundaries have changed over the years.

There is no single complete set of South Australian electoral rolls available for public consultation. For convenience, the various publicly available South Australian sources and their holdings are briefly mentioned here.

1884-1913

- South Australian electoral rolls for the period 1884-1913 [incomplete] for both the Legislative Council and House of Assembly are available on microfiche in the Family History Collection and at State Records (see page 81).

  There is a *Guide and index* to these South Australian electoral rolls 1884-1913. Prepared by Stathis Avramis, 1990. 1v.
  The index lists all polling places with their electoral divisions, and indicates which microfiche they appear on.

1905 onwards

- The Australian Electoral Commission (see page 70) holds South Australian electoral rolls from 1905 onwards.

1938-1989

- An incomplete set of South Australian electoral rolls in hardcopy from 1938-1989 is held in the Bray Reference Library (see pages 49-50).

1988 onwards

- From 1988 onwards the electoral rolls have been published in microfiche. The latest set is held in the Bray Reference Library (see pages 49-50). The rest are held in the Mortlock Library preservation collections – they are not on open access, but are still available for public use on request (see pages 53-54).

NATURALIZATION

Original naturalization records are held by the Australian Archives, Australian Capital Territory Office in Canberra. However, microfilm copies of South Australian certificates are held by the Australian Archives, South Australian Regional Office for the period 1848-1903 (see page 69).

The Family History Collection holds the following:

- *South Australia. Parliamentary paper. no. 147 (1872).*
  Lists aliens naturalized to 1872. Includes name, place of residence and occupation. The same list was also published in the *South Australian Government Gazette* of 15 August 1872.

- *Nominal index to South Australian naturalization records (1848-1903).* Compiled by the Australian Archives, ACT office. m/fiche.
  This index is arranged alphabetically by surname. Some useful notes on searching for particular surnames appear at the beginning.

The use of the term 'alien' to describe migrant groups of non-English speaking background is not acceptable in Australia today. However, archivists do not change original terms to reflect modern day attitudes. The terms in themselves provide an insight into the social outlook of the time.

[No. 147.

SOUTH AUSTRALIA.

—

ALIENS NATURALIZED TO JUNE, 1872.

Ordered by the House of Assembly to be printed, 13th August, 1872.

LIST of **PERSONS** who have **TAKEN** the **OATH** of **ALLEGIANCE** during the period from **the FOUNDATION** of the **COLONY** to June 30th, 1872.

Amsberg, Julius Michael, Adelaide, merchant	Bertheau, Carl Eduard, Adelaide, farmer
Amsberg, Benjamin, Adelaide, merchant	Beyer, August, Adelaide, storekeeper
Anders, Franz, Adelaide, carpenter	Blumner, Gotthilf Leberecht Hartmann, Glen Osmond, gardener
Almers, Louis, Adelaide, butcher	
Albert, Andreas, Rosenthal, farmer	Bungert, Johann Christian Gustav, Adelaide, butcher
Alexander, Moritz, Adelaide, merchant	Bayer, Frederick Charles, Adelaide, physician

Extract from South Australia. Parliamentary Paper no.147 *(1872).*

NEWSPAPER SOURCES

Newspapers can be a valuable source for establishing details of births, deaths, marriages, etc. However, owing to the limited availability of indexes, searching newspapers may prove a time-consuming task unless dates are determined as accurately as possible beforehand. The following indexes may be useful for finding information in South Australian newspapers:

- *Index to notices of births, deaths and marriages as well as obituaries published in certain South Australian newspapers for various periods between 1837-c.1936.* (Reference: Abbott Index). Card index + m/fiche. (m/fiche available for purchase : see page viii)
  Named after Frank Abbott who compiled this index. The cards are arranged alphabetically by name and give the newspaper reference and an abstract of the notice.

  The South Australian Genealogy and Heraldry Society Library (see pages 77-78) holds the Blair Index to pre-1900 birth, death and marriage entries in selected newspapers. This complements the Abbott Index.

- *Index to notices of births, deaths and marriages as well as obituaries appearing in South Australian Catholic newspapers for various periods between 1867-1945.* (Reference: Keain Index). Card index.
  Named after Maurice Keain who compiled this index. The cards are arranged alphabetically by name and give the newspaper reference and an abstract of the notice.

- *Register personal notices.* Edited by Reg Butler and Alan Phillips. Gumeracha, S. Aust. : Gould Books, c1989–. 3v.
  So far, this series covers all birth, death, marriage and other personal notices appearing in the *Register* newspaper from 1836 until 1870. All entries are reproduced in full, unless noted in the entry concerned. Indexes are provided so individual names can be searched.

- *Adelaide Observer index* covers the period 1880 to 1908. Two useful headings for the family historian are 'Biographical' and 'Obituary'.

- *Advertiser index* covers the period 1932 to 1966. It can be worth searching this index under the heading 'Obituary'.

- *PressCom Australia* is a database which contains most of the text of *The Advertiser, The News, The Sunday Mail*, Messenger Press and some interstate and overseas newspapers. Dates covered by the South Australian newspapers are as follows:

The Advertiser	(from Jan. 1986)
The News	(Jan. 1989 - Mar. 1992)
Sunday Mail	(from Aug. 1988)
Messenger Press	(from Jan. 1989)

  It should be noted that the database does not contain graphics, charts, tables, or birth, death and marriage notices. Staff carry out *PressCom* searches as required. For further details, ask at the Bray Reference Library desk.

PAPERS RELATIVE TO THE

Statement of the Extent and Cultivation of

DISTRICT A.—*continued*.

No. of Section.	Name of Place or Farm.	Name of Cultivator.	Wheat.	Barley.	Oats.	Maize.	Potatoes.	Garden.	Supplied with Water, and how.
. .	Port Adelaide . .	South Australian Company and others.	.	.	.	.	.	.	From a well 14 feet deep, including four feet of good water.
. .	Albert Town . . .	. .	.	.	.	.	.	.	From the Half-way House, on the Adelaide road.
P. 238	Unley Village . .	T. Whistler and others .	.	.	.	.	.	.	From several wells, from 30 to 40 feet below the surface. Good water.
. .	Reed Beds . . .	Charles Sturt . . .	.	.	.	.	.	.	Well, five feet deep, including four feet of water.
426	. .	Wm. Garlick and others .	.	.	.	.	.	.	Two wells, one 17 feet deep, including four feet of water; and the other, 21 feet deep, containing three feet of water.
425	Miners' Village . .	John Rowe and others .	.	.	.	.	.	.	Three wells, each 16 feet deep, including three feet of water.
424	Freeman's Place .	Bell Freeman and others	.	.	.	.	.	.	Three wells, each 22 feet deep, including four feet of water.
P. 409	Tenterden, or Half-way House.	R. Cunningham & others	.	.	.	.	.	.	Well, 20 feet deep, including four feet of water.
P. 405	. .	Aaron Brien, tenant of Captain Lipson.	.	.	.	.	.	.	. .
. .	. .	Thomas Whistler . .	.	.	.	.	.	.	Well, 28 feet deep, including five feet of water.
P. 424	. .	Benjamin Stone . . .	.	.	.	.	.	.	From the Half-way Houses. Water found on this section is salt.
379, 392, and 397.	Tam O'Shanter Land	Wm. Burridge and others	.	.	.	.	.	4½	Five wells, each 23 feet deep, including three feet of water.
393, 394	Pennington . . .	Jos. Pentridge and others	.	.	.	.	.	.	. .
. .	. .	John Cowled	.	.	.	.	.	.	. .
350	. .	Captain Ellis and others.	4	.	.	.	.	.	Well, 98 feet deep, including six feet of water.
½ P. 349	. .	Joseph Ind	1½	¾	.	4	2	.	From the Torrens . . . .

Details of cultivators and their land holdings as provided in Official Statistical Returns relative to the progress of the colony of South Australia, at the termination of the year 1840.

PAPERS RELATIVE TO SOUTH AUSTRALIA

In the early years of white settlement, a number of papers relative to the colonies in Australia appeared in the British Parliamentary Papers. One of these is:

- *Papers relative to South Australia presented to both Houses of Parliament by command of Her Majesty*. London : HMSO, 1843.

  Of particular interest from these papers are the 'Official Statistical Returns relative to the progress of the colony of South Australia, at the termination of the year 1840'. (Included within (no.39) no.17. Copy of a Despatch from Governor Grey to Lord John Russell, Government House, Adelaide, 7 October, 1841. pages 70-101).

  Copies of these pages are located in the Family History Collection, under the title *Papers relative to South Australia.*

  An alternative location is the Bray Reference Library where they are held in *British Parliamentary Papers: Colonies: Australia; Sessions 1816-1899*. Irish University Press series of British Parliamentary Papers. Shannon : Irish University Press, 1968-70. Sessions 1842-44, Volume 7, pages 100-131.

  As the division into districts used in these returns corresponds with those of the 1841 census (see page 22), they can be used together. For example, if you have established that a person was a cultivator in a particular district from the 1841 census, then you might find further information regarding the 'Extent and Cultivation of Land, Supply of Water, Remarks on Crops and Buildings', by searching through the lists of cultivators for that district.

  The boundaries of the various districts are shown on: Arrowsmith, John. *Map showing the Special Surveys in South Australia to the Eastward of the Gulf of St. Vincent from documents in the Survey Office Adelaide*. London : John Arrowsmith, 1 March 1841. It is held in the Map Collection (see pages 51-52).

  Papers relative to South Australia are indexed in *Colonial residents of South Australia 1839-1848* which also shows all of the information from the relevant entry (see page 23).

PORTRAITS

The Mortlock Library's Pictorial Collection contains over 70,000 photographs (see pages 58-59). This collection is the first place to check for portraits. However the Family History Collection contains a number of indexes to sources of portraits of early European settlers in South Australia:

- *List of people arriving in South Australia from overseas ports. 1836-1845* (Reference 1048, see page 33). The list is indexed. Included in the unofficial sources which were used to compile the list, are the following:

  Source 45   *South Australian pioneers, 1838–*: [portrait photographs]. By T. Duryea. (B7864).

  Source 46   *South Australian pioneers, 1840*: [portrait photographs]. By T. Duryea. (B7865).

  Source 47   *Old colonists banquet group*: (most of whom attended a banquet given by Mr. Emanuel Solomon, 28 December, 1871). [portrait photographs]. By H. Jones. (B7677). (Also referred to as OCJ).

  Source 48   *Old colonists, 1836-40*: [portrait photographs]. By T. Duryea. (B8235). (Also referred to as OCD).

  Source 49   *Group of old colonists:* [women]. (Most of whom arrived before 1841). By H. Jones. (B19985).

  Sources 46-49 also have their own individual surname indexes. It should be noted that most of the groups are artificially arranged. Individual portraits have been brought together to form a composite group photograph.

Portraits of people also appear in published sources, for example, newspapers, periodicals and books. Biographical indexes to published sources are located near the Mortlock Library reference desk. Ask staff for assistance.

COPYING

A photographic print service is available from the State Library's Image Centre for individual portraits included in these sources (see page viii).

South Australian pioneers 1840 *as photographed by T. Duryea. SSL:M:B7865*

SHIPPING AND PASSENGER LISTS

INTRODUCTION

These shipping and passenger lists cover only those arrivals and departures which were to or from South Australia.

Many of the lists are copies of official Government records.

Many of the official passenger lists have not survived or have been destroyed. Some unofficial passenger lists have been compiled from a variety of sources, including newspapers.

This section has been arranged in chronological order under the following headings:

SHIPPING AND PASSENGER ARRIVALS

- Arrivals from interstate
- Arrivals from overseas

SHIPPING AND PASSENGER DEPARTURES

- Departures for interstate
- Departures for overseas

GENERAL SHIPPING SOURCES

SHIPPING PHOTOGRAPHS

Clipper ship 'Orient' which first arrived in South Australia from London in September 1856, and made yearly trips until 1877. This ship was the foundation of the 'Orient' line of sail and steam ships. SSL:M:B1777

SHIPPING AND PASSENGER ARRIVALS

Arrivals from Interstate

1837-November 1859

*   *Index to passenger lists published in South Australian newspapers of arrivals in South
    Australian ports from interstate and New Zealand. 1837-Nov. 1859.* (Reference: Hodge
    Index). Card index + m/fiche. (m/fiche available for purchase : see page viii)
    The index is arranged alphabetically by name of passenger. It gives name of the ship,
    master of the ship and date of arrival. References are given to the newspaper/s where the
    name appears.

December 1859 onwards

*   No indexes or official passenger lists for this period are available in the State Library.

Arrivals from Overseas

1836-1845

*   *Lists of people arriving in South Australia from overseas ports. 1836-1845.* (Reference
    number: 1048. Original at State Records GRG 56/68/5). 35v. [incl. *index & key*].
    These lists are incomplete and were compiled from many different agencies, largely
    from unofficial sources. The amount of data supplied is very limited and varies
    according to the compiler. The sources are arranged numerically and often do not give
    forenames or initials, names of wives and children, place of origin or age, and
    frequently do not indicate family relationships.

    Index: There is an index volume to all the sources used. It is arranged alphabetically by
    name of passenger. 1v. + m/film, 1 reel.

    '*Key*' *to index*: The key gives the number of the particular source/s where the name
    appears. 1v. + m/film, 1 reel. [Includes *Chronological list of ships arriving in South
    Australia from overseas. 1836-1845*. (Reference number: 997. Original at State Records
    GRG 56/68/4)].

*   Source 25: *Manifest books of vessels arriving at Port Adelaide from overseas and
    interstate ports, with lists of crew 1838-1842*. (Reference number: 743. Original at State
    Records GRG 41/8). 3v. + m/film, 1 reel. [Especially useful as it includes crew lists;
    crew names are not included in the index to 1048 which is only to passengers; for other
    records relating to crew see Australian Archives, South Australian Regional Office (see
    page 69)].

*   *Official passenger lists mainly of immigrants arriving in South Australia under United
    Kingdom assisted passage schemes. 1845*. (Reference number: 313. Original at State
    Records GRG 35/48A). 1v. + m/film.
    The lists are **not** indexed. They refer to the two ships the 'Isabella Watson' which
    arrived on 4 April 1845 and the 'Templar' which arrived on 24 November 1845.

Arrivals from Overseas

1846-1887

- *Official passenger lists mainly of immigrants arriving in South Australia under United Kingdom assisted passage schemes. 1847-1886.* (Reference number: 313. Original at State Records GRG 35/48A). 30v. + m/film, 9 reels + m/fiche. (m/fiche available for purchase : see page viii)

  Not all lists have survived but available lists give passengers' names, most give ages, occupation and marital status, while some also give county of origin. Passenger lists held in England relating to these voyages were destroyed in 1900.

  Index: The index to the passenger lists is arranged alphabetically by name of passenger, and gives the reference to the passenger list/s where the name appears. A chronological listing of the passenger lists appears at the beginning of both volumes, giving the list reference number and name of ship. 2v. (m/fiche available for purchase : see page viii)

  A number of abbreviations are used in conjunction with these shipping lists. The classifications of emigrants are as shown. Although not completely certain, it is believed that religious denominations are as shown.

Classifications of Emigrants

C.P.C.	Colonial Passage Certificate
C.F.P.	Colonial Full Paid Passage
U.K.A.P.	United Kingdom Assisted Passage
U.K.F.P.	United Kingdom Full Paid Passage
F.P.	United Kingdom Free Passage (from 313 76/19 frame 4)

Religious Denominations

E.	Church of England
C.	Catholic
D.	Dissenter
S.	Scots? (Presbyterian)
F.	Free Mason
M.	Methodist
P.	Presbyterian
W.	Wesleyan
B.	Baptist
I.	Independent

Extract from a copy of the official passenger list for the 'Shackamaxon' which arrived in Port Adelaide on 19 January 1853.

Photograph courtesy of State Records.

- *Official passenger lists of immigrants arriving in South Australia from Hamburg. 1851, 1855-1886.* (Reference number: 1531). 3v. [commonly known as Hamburg Index] Lists record passengers' names, place of residence, age, occupation, sex and age grouping of family. Not all lists have survived nor are our holdings complete. Some German arrivals are listed in *Official passenger lists mainly of immigrants arriving in South Australia under United Kingdom assisted passage schemes. 1847-1886* (see above) and in the *Index to passenger lists of ships arriving in South Australia from overseas published in newspapers. 1846-1887* (see below).

  Index: There is an index for the period 1855-1886 arranged alphabetically by name. Reference is given to red page numbers in the volumes. The index is to the head of a household, usually male, although families are fully listed in the volumes. Card index.

- *Passenger lists from Hamburg to Port Adelaide for the 'San Francisco' departed 15 June 1850, 'Sophie' departed 25 April 1850, and 'Dockenhuden' departed 20 October 1850.* 1v.
  These lists are reproduced from the publication *German and Central European emigration. Monograph no.1, Parts 1 & 3. Reconstructed passenger lists for 1850: Hamburg to Australia, Brazil, Canada, Chile and the United States.* Edited by C.N. Smith. McNeal, Arizona : Westland Publications, 1980.

- *Index to passenger lists of ships arriving in South Australia from overseas published in newspapers. 1846-1887.* (Reference: 'Newspaper Index'). 5v. [incl. key].
  The passenger lists appearing in newspapers are very incomplete but include many unassisted passengers and German immigrants. Personal details about individuals are rarely given and forenames and initials are often omitted. The index cites coded references to the relevant newspaper and year and is arranged alphabetically by name. To obtain the exact reference, the *Key* to the index must be consulted.

  Key to index: The key to the index volumes indicates the exact date of the newspaper where the passenger list appears and gives the name of the ship. All the newspaper titles indexed are available on microfilm. 1v.

1888-1940

- *Official lists of people arriving in South Australia from overseas. 1888-1940.* (Reference number: 764. Original at State Records GRG 41/34). m/film, 28 reels. This material is arranged chronologically with each ship's list held for the relevant years. Holdings are incomplete.

  There is an index to passengers for the period 1888-1908. (Reference: Burdett Index) m/fiche. Accompanying this source is a chronological list of the ships for which passenger lists are held. 1v.

Arrivals from Overseas

1925-1956

- A passenger index covering the period 1925-1956 is a feature of the computer database of passenger arrivals at the South Australian Maritime Museum (see page 78).
  A copy of this index is available on microfiche and in hard copy in the Family History Collection. This index was compiled from sources held at the State Library for the period 1925-1940, and from passenger lists 1941- which are held at the Australian Archives, South Australian Regional Office (see page 69).

SHIPPING AND PASSENGER DEPARTURES

Departures for Interstate

1837-1859

- *Index to passenger lists published in South Australian newspapers of departures from South Australian ports for interstate and New Zealand. 1837-Nov. 1859.* (Reference: Hodge Index). Card index + m/fiche. (m/fiche available for purchase : see page viii)
  The index is arranged alphabetically by name of passenger. It gives name of the ship, master of the ship and date of arrival. References are given to the newspaper/s where the name appears.

1860 onwards

- No indexes or official passenger lists for this period are available at the State Library.

Departures for Overseas

1836-1887

- *Index to departures by ship from South Australia for overseas (not intra or interstate) from the Register newspaper. 1836-1887.* (Reference: Horner Index). Card index + m/fiche. (m/fiche available for purchase : see page viii)

  Named after Sally Horner who compiled the index. The cards are arranged alphabetically by passenger's name, in two sequences 1836-1875, 1876-1887. Entries give: name of ship, master of ship, date of departure and route information if available. References are given to the issue of the *Register* where the name appears.

1888-1910

- *Official lists of people departing from Port Adelaide for overseas ports. 1888-1910.* (Reference number: 766. Original at State Records GRG 41/35). m/film, 4 reels.

  This material is arranged chronologically. Holdings are incomplete. There is no index to passengers but there is a chronological list of the ships for which passenger lists are held. If you have a specific ship in mind you can check the list under the relevant year/s to see whether the ship's official passenger list is held. 1v.

Departures for Overseas

1911-1940

- **No** official passenger lists or indexes for this period are available at the State Library. Departure lists for the period 1911-1940 are held by State Records (see pages 80-81).

1940 onwards

- **No** official passenger lists or indexes for this period are available at the State Library. Departure lists for the period 1941-1964 are held at the Australian Archives, South Australian Regional Office (see page 69).

GENERAL SHIPPING SOURCES

- *Index to immigrant ships referred to in archival sources such as diaries and other records. 1836-1900.* (Reference: Immigrant Ship Index). Card index.

  The index is arranged alphabetically by name of ship. It gives the record number of the material which contains a reference to the particular ship. Records referred to are held either by the Mortlock Library or State Records (see page 80-81). Staff can help you determine the location of specific items.

- *Index to ships arriving in South Australia from overseas. 1836-1900.* (Reference number: 908. Original at State Records GRG 56/68/1). 2v.

  The index is arranged alphabetically by name of ship, and includes references to the existence of passenger lists and the date the ship arrived.

There are other general indexes to archival and published material that include references to ships' voyages. A number of books have been published about early ships and these may include details of passenger arrivals. These publications may be found by referring to the State Library catalogues.

SHIPPING PHOTOGRAPHS

There is little likelihood of a **photograph** existing for ships prior to 1875. (See the preface to *Migrant ships for South Australia 1836-1860* by Ronald Parsons. Gumeracha, SA : Gould Books, c1988.)

The Mortlock Library of South Australiana ships collection is available on videodisk (see page 59).

Major shipping collections and additional indexes to illustrations of ships are held in the Rare Books and Named Collections of the State Library of South Australia (see page 60-61).

INTERSTATE AND OVERSEAS SOURCES

The Family History Collection not only contains specifically South Australian material, but also guides, indexes and copies of sources to do with people from interstate and overseas. Initially 500 titles were transferred from the Bray Reference Library and new sources are being added regularly. The latest major addition is the 1992 edition of the *International genealogical index*.

This section provides an overview of some important areas covered, lists some examples, and suggests ways to find further information. It should also be noted that there are numerous other sources for family history still held in the Bray Reference Library (see pages 49-50).

The following topics are covered in this section:
      Army records
      Biographical sources
      Births, deaths and marriages
      Directories and almanacs
      Harleian Collection
      Heraldry
      International Genealogical Index
      Irish Transportation Records
      Shipping records

Ms Sally Horner and Mrs Patricia Horner consulting a reference from the Family History Collection.

ARMY RECORDS

There are a number of publications in the Family History Collection that list army records, including militia lists from England and many items covering World War I and World War II. The collection is strongest for Great Britain and Australia. Examples of the kinds of material that may be found are:

- *Annual British Army lists 1740-1784.* Wakefield, England : Microform Academic Publishers, 1984. m/fiche.

- Kitzmiller, John W. *In search of the 'forlorn hope'.* Salt Lake City, Utah : Manuscript Pub. Foundation, c1988. 3v. This is a guide to locating British regiments and their records from 1640 onwards.

- *Nominal roll of A.I.F. who left Australia for service abroad, 1914-1918 war.* [Canberra : Australian War Memorial, 1987?]. m/fiche.

- Pemberton, Gregory. *Vietnam remembered.* Sydney : Weldon Publishing, 1990. This contains the names of all Australians who fought in Vietnam.

- *Roll call! A guide to genealogical sources in the Australian War Memorial.* Canberra : Australian War Memorial, 1988. Provides information on records held by the Australian War Memorial and other organisations.

Two useful subject headings for those wishing to check the State Library catalogues for further information are:

Australia. Australian Army – Registers
Great Britain. Army – Registers

A number of other sources are held in the collections of the Bray Reference Library (see pages 49-50). Do not hesitate to ask library staff for assistance.

BIOGRAPHICAL SOURCES

The Family History Collection holds numerous items containing biographical information. For non-South Australian states, and overseas, examples include:

Censuses

- *1831 census County Londonderry*. Derry, Northern Ireland : Inner City Trust, [1989]. m/fiche.

- *Census of New South Wales, November 1828*. Edited by Malcolm R. Sainty & Keith A. Johnson. Sydney : Library of Australian History, 1980.

Dictionaries of biography

- *The Bicentennial dictionary of Western Australians, pre-1829-1888*. General editor: Rica Erickson. Nedlands, WA : University of Western Australia, 1987–.

- *Biographical register of the Australian Capital Territory, 1820-1911*. Edited by Eunice Fletcher. Canberra : Heraldry & Genealogy Society of Canberra, 1993.

Ships' captains

- *Lloyd's captains' registers, 1851-1947*. London, World Microfilm Publications, 1987. m/film.

Muster lists and militia lists [mainly England]

- Gibson, J.S.W. and Medlycott, M. *Militia lists and musters, 1757-1876: a directory of holdings in the British Isles*. 2nd ed. Birmingham, England : Federation of Family History Societies, 1990.

- *Oxfordshire militia ballot, 1831: City of Oxford, hundreds of Bullingdon, Thame and Dorchester*. Oxford, [England] : Oxfordshire Family History Society, c1989.

Police records

- *Victoria police gazette [1853-1870]*. Melbourne, Vic. : Library Council of Victoria, 1989. m/fiche.

These examples provide a sampling of resources. Check catalogues, or ask staff to find whether the library holds other material relevant to your needs.

BIRTHS, DEATHS AND MARRIAGES

INTERSTATE

Indexes to births, deaths and marriages records are held in microform for NSW, Northern Territory, Queensland, Tasmania, Victoria and Western Australia. The Tasmanian records on microfilm contain indexes to the Registers and – from 1803 to 1899 – **copies of the complete record**. Miscellaneous Northern Territory records have been compiled from original records and supplement the indexes. Family History Source Sheet no.4. *A list of interstate births, deaths and marriages records and indexes on microform* is updated regularly and gives the most recent listing of holdings. In summary the index coverage is as follows:

- New South Wales

Baptisms	pre 1856
Births	1856-1905
Burials	pre 1856
Deaths	1856-1905
Marriages	pre 1856
Marriages	1856-1905

- Northern Territory

Births	1870-1902
Deaths	1870-1902
Marriages	1870-1902

- Queensland

Baptisms	1829-1856
Births	1850-1904
Burials	1829-1856
Deaths	1895-1904
Marriages	1839-1904
Marriages	1856-1893
(Country marriages)	

- Tasmania

Baptisms	1803-1933
Births	1838-1899
Burials	1803-1933
Deaths	1838-1899
Marriages	1803-1838
(Pre civil registration)	
Marriages	1838-1899

- Victoria

Births	1853-1913
Deaths	1854-1960
Marriages	1853-1930

- Western Australia

Births	1841-1905
Deaths	1841-1905
Marriages	1841-1905

- *Pioneer indexes* held on CD-ROM provide further sources for interstate births, deaths and marriages. The disks for Victoria and Tasmania cover pre-civil registration church records and continue until 1888 for Victoria, and 1899 for Tasmania. The New South Wales records are being produced in two parts; so far only the Federation Series 1889-1918 is available. Earlier records dating from 1788-1888 are still being compiled.

Various other indexes have been published, including:

- *Index to birth, marriage, death & funeral notices in the Sydney Morning Herald.* Compiled by Malcolm R. Sainty & Keith A. Johnson. Sydney : Genealogical Publications of Australia, 1973-1975. 4v.

- *Whitton's index to the [Hobart] Mercury.* Compiled by K. & A. Whitton. Hobart : GST Inc., Hobart Branch, 1993. 3v.: v.1. Birth notices, 1858-1899 (incomplete); v.2. Marriage notices, 1858-1899 (incomplete); v.3. Death notices, 1858-1899 (incomplete).

OVERSEAS

See page 45. *International genealogical index.*
See page 43. Harleian Collection.

The Family History Collection also contains many items relating to wills and parish registers – particularly those located in England and Ireland. Examples are:

- *Index to Surrey wills proved in the Prerogative Court of Canterbury, 1650-1700.* Edited by Cliff Webb. Woking, Surrey, England : West Surrey Family History Society, c1989.

- Phillimore, W.P.W. and Thrift, G. *Indexes to Irish wills.* Baltimore, MD : Genealogical Publishing Co., 1970.

- *Wills and where to find them.* Compiled by J.S.W. Gibson. Chichester, England : Phillimore, Published for the British Record Society, 1974.

Mrs Laurel Young, Councillor of the South Australian Genealogy and Heraldry Society, and Mr Bill Young using the Victorian Pioneer Index *on CD-ROM.*

DIRECTORIES AND ALMANACS

The collection of interstate directories and almanacs covers all states and the Australian Capital Territory. Family History Source Sheet no.5. *Interstate almanacs and directories held in the State Library of South Australia* gives a comprehensive listing of the library's holdings.

The library is currently receiving microfiche copies of nineteenth century directories for various English counties. An up-to-date listing of these holdings can be found in Family History Source Sheet no.8. *Interstate/Overseas sources on microform.*

HARLEIAN COLLECTION

The Harleian Society, which was founded in 1869, is a learned society formed to transcribe, print and publish heraldic visitations of counties, parish registers and any manuscripts relating to family history, genealogy or heraldry.

The State Library has been subscribing to these publications since the nineteenth century and holds a complete set of the society's volumes. These list the names of many thousands of individuals dating back to the fourteenth century.

Included in this collection are several hundred volumes of Public Record Office records from the National Archives (Great Britain), including items such as *Calendar of Patent Rolls* and *Close Rolls*, dating from the thirteenth and fourteenth centuries.

Most of the volumes in this collection are indexed alphabetically with references to people, places or subjects mentioned.

These volumes cover England only.

More detailed notes on this collection are available in the Family History Collection.

HERALDRY

The Family History Collection contains a number of volumes on heraldry. The collection is strongest in works to do with Great Britain. Examples of holdings are:

General works such as

- Fox-Davies, A.C. *A complete guide to heraldry.* London : Orbis, 1985.

- Papworth, J.W. *An alphabetical dictionary of coats of arms.* Baltimore, MD : Genealogical Publishing Company, 1965.

Specific works include

- *Burke's genealogical and heraldic history of the landed gentry.* 1st ed. (1834-1838) – . Imperfect.

- *Burke's genealogical and heraldic history of the peerage, baronetage and knightage* 1859–. Imperfect.

The Royal Arms of Great Britain.

- *Fairbairn's crests of the families of Great Britain and Ireland.* Revised by Laurence Butters. Edinburgh : A. Fullarton & Co., 1896. 2v.

There are also many items in the collections of the Bray Reference Library (see pages 49-50).

The only authentic source of information on British coats of arms is The College of Arms, Queen Victoria Street, London EC4V 4BT.

Pedigrees

The Harleian Collection (see page 43) contains many pedigrees.

Pedigrees are also held for some European countries including Germany, Poland and Italy. Examples are:

- Niesiecki, Kasper. *Herbarz polski Kaspra Niesieckiego S.J. / powiekszony dodatkami z pozniejszych autorow, rekopismow, dowodow urzedowych i wydany przez Jana Nep. Bobrowicza.* Warszawa : Wydawnictwa Artystyczne i Filmowe, 1979. 10v. [Reprint. Originally published: W Lipsku : Breitkopf i Haertel, 1839-1846].

- Spreti, Vittorio. *Enciclopedia storico-nobiliare.* Sala, Bolognese : Arnoldo Forni Editore, 1981. 8v.

The work of Albrecht Durer from Fox-Davies, A.C. The art of heraldry. New York : Benjamin Bloom Inc., 1968.

INTERNATIONAL GENEALOGICAL INDEX (IGI)

The *International genealogical index* (1992 edition. m/fiche.) is an index compiled by the Family History Library of the Church of Jesus Christ of Latter-Day Saints. The index lists christenings and marriages from sources including wills, census records, compiled marriage indexes and LDS church members' research. There are 187,000,000 names listed from over 145 countries covering a time span from the early fifteenth century to 1875.

A finding aid to the index has been produced by the State Library of South Australia. This lists fiche number, region, locality and last name on the fiche.

IRISH TRANSPORTATION RECORDS

The *Irish transportation records of convicts transported to Australia between 1788 and 1856* were a bicentennial gift from the Government and people of Ireland to the Government and people of Australia and are part of the Australian Joint Copying Project. The Family History Collection has its own permanent copy of these records consisting of a computer index that must be consulted before a specific convict's record can be located, and copies of the original records which are stored on 105 microfilms. The index is located on the Family History Collection workstation.

It is important to note that these records refer to the **convicts only**. Not all of the Chief Secretary's Office records survive, especially for the period before 1836, but there is sufficient material to make Irish archives a major source for Australians researching their Irish ancestors. A successful search in the records may produce not just a bald official summary, but perhaps one of the thousands of petitions for commutation or remission of sentence submitted by or on behalf of the prisoner.

For further information see State Library of South Australia. Family History Research Guide no.3. *Irish transportation records*.

SHIPPING RECORDS

The largest listing of arrivals to ports other than South Australian are the *Irish transportation records* (see page 45). Other items provide shipping information or list the arrivals of particular groups such as convicts. Examples are:

- *Argus passenger index 1846-1860.* Gisborne, Vic. : M. Button, 1992. m/fiche.

- *Immigration to Victoria: index to inward passenger lists, foreign ports 1852-1859.* Melbourne : Public Record Office, 1993. m/fiche.

- Schenk, Trudy et al. *The Wuerttemberg emigration index.* Salt Lake City, Utah : Ancestry Inc., 1986-. 5v.

- Tardif, Phillip. *Notorious strumpets and dangerous girls.* NSW : Angus & Robertson, 1990. (This gives a physical description of the women convicts listed.)

For further information see Family History Source Sheet no.9. *Interstate/Overseas passenger lists and immigrant registers.*

In most instances if you are searching the arrival of an ancestor to an interstate port you will need to contact the archival institution of that State for information (see pages 84-87).

PART 3

THE BRAY AND MORTLOCK LIBRARIES AND SPECIAL COLLECTIONS

Computerisation enables efficient searching of the State Library's published material catalogued since 1981, and various databases. In the future the card catalogues and indexes will be transferred onto the on-line catalogue.

BRAY REFERENCE LIBRARY

Location:	Bastyan Wing State Library of South Australia North Terrace Adelaide 5000
Postal address:	GPO Box 419 Adelaide 5001

Telephone:

Enquiries	(08) 207 7250
	(08) 207 7252
SA country callers	008 182 013
TTY	(08) 207 7251
Fax	(08) 207 7247

PC access: Users with a personal computer, modem, and communications software can dial-in to SALINET, the computerised component of the library's catalogue. Telephone the help desk on (08) 207 7328 during library hours for details

Hours: Monday to Friday 9.30 am to 8.00 pm
Saturday, Sunday 12.00 pm to 5.00 pm
Closed on public holidays

The Bray Reference Library is a general reference and research library for all South Australians. It contains hundreds of thousands of books, magazines, newspapers, indexes, dictionaries and encyclopaedias covering a huge range of subjects. Staff are available to assist with enquiries ranging from ready reference to more detailed research. The collection has been built up over more than a hundred years. Many of the items are relevant to family history research. Among the more important are:

AJCP

- *Australian Joint Copying Project.* No.1–. 1948–. Imperfect. m/film.
  Established under an agreement signed by the National Library of Australia and the State Library of New South Wales jointly to microfilm material in the Public Record Office, London and elsewhere relating to Australia and the Pacific. Some items contain convict records.

Biographical material

- *Australian dictionary of biography.*
- *Dictionary of national biography.*
- *Who's who.* [These are published for many countries, including Australia, Great Britain, and United States of America.]

Electoral Rolls

- Some electoral rolls are held from all states, the Australian Capital Territory and the Northern Territory. The library's holdings are incomplete, but beginning dates are as follows. Note that although most are held in the Bray Reference Library, some South Australian and Northern Territory electoral rolls are in the Mortlock Library or Family History Collection (see page 25).

Australian Capital Territory	1937
New South Wales	1858
Northern Territory	1931 (a single roll for Palmerston, 1895 is also held)
Queensland	1958
South Australia	1884
Tasmania	1960
Victoria	1959
Western Australia	1958

Heraldry and Pedigrees

- *Debrett's Peerage and Baronetage.*
- *Reitstap's Planches de l'Armorial General.*

Newspapers

- All the major Australian and some major overseas newspapers are held.

- Newspaper indexes include:
  The Argus [Melbourne]. 1846-1949.
  Sydney Morning Herald. 1900-1914; 1927-1987. some m/fiche.
  The New York Times. 1941–.
  The Times [London]. 1790–.

- Increasingly the text of newspapers is becoming available in the form of electronic databases, which can be searched by key words. However they frequently do not cover birth, death and marriage notices. For particular information about particular newspapers, seek advice from staff.

Periodicals

- *Almanach de Gotha.* 1847-1937. Imperfect.
- *Crockford's clerical directory.* 1882–. Imperfect.
- *Gentleman's Magazine.* 1731-1907.
- *Great Britain. War Office. The army list.* 1924-42; 1949–. Imperfect.
- *Great Britain. War Office. Navy list.* 1914–. Imperfect.
- *Notes and queries.* 1849/50–.

County Histories

- *Victoria history of the counties of England.* This is a continuing series. Check the catalogues for up-to-date details of county histories held.

MAP COLLECTION

The State Library of South Australia Map Collection is available to the public during all State Library opening hours. Enquiries should be directed to the Reference Library enquiry desk where a trained librarian can assist you. The Map Collection has extensive mapping, gazetteers, atlases, and related resources to help the family history researcher.
Some examples are:

- Complete sets of nineteenth century mapping and related gazetteers for England, Wales, Ireland and Scotland at the 1:63,360 scale.

- A comprehensive collection of mapping for Germany and Prussia at the 1:100,000 and 1:200,000 scales, an incomplete set of Landkries maps at the 1:100,000 scale, plus related gazetteers and atlases.

- Australian mapping is held at the national scale of 1:250,000 and all the states at 1:100,000 and either 1:50,000 or 1:25,000 scales. Both current and older mapping are held.

- An extensive collection of South Australian hundreds and county maps (covering a wide date span from the mid nineteenth century to the present), pastoral plans and series mapping at various scales, and a large collection of town plans. Location-finding resources such as gazetteers and place name books are also available.

A selection of specific historical South Australian mapping which may assist family history researchers is listed below:

- Arrowsmith, John. *The district of Adelaide, South Australia, as divided into country sections, from the trigonometrical surveys of Colonel Light late Survr. General.* London : John Arrowsmith, 18 Feb. 1839.
  Purchasers' names are shown on sold sections.

- Arrowsmith, John. *Map showing the Special Surveys in South Australia to the Eastward of the Gulf of St. Vincent from documents in the Survey Office Adelaide.* London : John Arrowsmith, 1 Mar. 1841.
  Shows the 32 Special Surveys and the Sections A, B, C, D, E, F which are used in the 1841 census (see page 22) and the *Papers relative to South Australia* (see page 29).

- Frearson, Robert S. *Map of South Australia and the Northern Territory shewing pastoral leases and claims.* [Adelaide] : Frearson, for *Pictorial Australian*, 1892.

- Light, William. *Plan of the city of Adelaide shewing the number of each [town] acre and the names of the streets, the name of the purchaser and the price. 27th and 28th March, 1837.* [From original plan of the Surveyor-General Wm. Light, Esq., 1837]. Adelaide : Surveyor General's Office [and] A. Vaughan, Govt. Photolithographer, [1890-1920]. Facsimile : M.E. Sharrah [1949-54].

- *Map of northern runs.* Lithographed in accordance with resolution of Legislative Council, 6th March 1866. Adelaide : Surveyor General's Office, 1866.

- Smith, Charles W. *Hydraulic Engineers Office, city survey, 80ft. to an inch. North Adelaide [and South Adelaide].* [Survey and plan of the city of Adelaide; prepared in connection with the drainage of the city and for information of the Land and Titles Office ... Work started by Mr Hyndman and carried out by C.W. Smith.] Adelaide : Surveyor General's Office, [1880?].
  Often called 'Smith's Survey' after Charles Smith [City Engineer]. Shows building names.

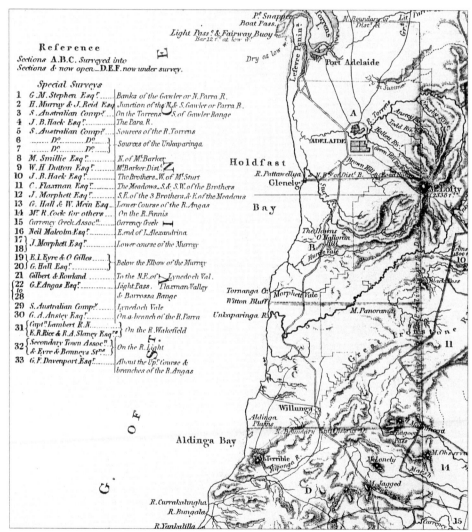

Detail from: Arrowsmith, John. Map showing the Special Surveys in South Australia to the Eastward of the Gulf of St. Vincent from documents in the Survey Office Adelaide. *London : John Arrowsmith, 1 Mar. 1841.*

MORTLOCK LIBRARY OF SOUTH AUSTRALIANA

Location:	Jervois Wing
	State Library of South Australia
	North Terrace
	Adelaide 5000
Postal address:	GPO Box 419
	Adelaide 5001

Telephone:	Enquiries	(08) 207 7360
	SA country callers	008 182 013
	TTY	(08) 207 7251
	Fax	(08) 207 7247

PC access:	Users with a personal computer, modem, and communications software can dial-in to SALINET, the computerised component of the library's catalogue. Telephone the help desk on (08) 207 7328 during library hours for details
Hours:	Monday to Friday 9.30 am to 8.00 pm
	Saturday, Sunday 12.00 pm to 5.00 pm
	Closed on public holidays

The Mortlock Library of South Australiana was established within the State Library in 1986, when important archival and published collections relating to South Australia, and developed over many years, were brought together. These collections document South Australia from before white settlement to the present day, and the Northern Territory to 1911.

The library has a national responsibility to collect, preserve and give access to historical and contemporary information covering topics such as South Australia's people, geography, architecture, environment, economy, political life, cultural pursuits, and scientific achievements.

Some points to bear in mind

- Mortlock material is not for loan and very little is on direct open access.
- More time needs to be allowed when using the Mortlock Library than would be required when using a local lending library.
- Preservation material requires careful handling. Users must observe certain procedures.
- Most of the records can be consulted by researchers once they have acquired a reader's pass (available on application).
- Preservation materials are only available for consultation in the Historical Treasures Reading Room.
- Copying of material is subject to the physical condition of the items and the normal provisions of copyright law.

Collections

The library holds material in a wide range of formats and in different languages. New items are received every day, including: books, maps, pamphlets, diaries, newspapers, business records, government publications, photographs, theatre programmes, oral history tapes, menus, films and artworks.

Legislation ensures that the Mortlock Library receives all material published in South Australia, including audio-visual material and computer disks. If you are publishing in South Australia please check with staff regarding legal deposit requirements (see page 5).

Materials of an archival nature such as family, business or society records, oral history tapes and photographs are largely received through donation. For valuable donations, the Mortlock Library is a registered institution under the Commonwealth's 'Taxation Incentives for the Arts' scheme. Leaflets about this scheme are available.

We appeal to all South Australians, or those with South Australian connections, who may hold archival or published material relating to South Australia, to seek advice from staff before disposing of items.

How we can help you

The Mortlock Library is open to the general public. Staff are available to assist with enquiries ranging from ready reference to more detailed research.

Notes for family historians

- The Mortlock Library collects material about people and places in South Australia. For the lives of interstate and overseas people, you will probably need to search elsewhere. (See interstate and overseas sources in the Family History Collection on pages 38-46 and the list of important interstate and overseas addresses on pages 84-88.)
- Some materials are held for the Northern Territory which was annexed to South Australia in 1863. As it became part of the Commonwealth of Australia on 1 January 1912, the Mortlock Library does not collect material relating to the Northern Territory after this date.
- The Mortlock Library does not hold official records of State Government departments and agencies. Copies of some shipping and immigration records are held in the Family History Collection. Many Local Government and State Government records are held at State Records (see pages 80-81).

The following pages highlight some important collections of the Mortlock Library of particular relevance for family historians. For a more detailed description of the Mortlock collections, refer to the illustrated *Guide to the collections: Mortlock Library of South Australiana*, Adelaide : Libraries Board of South Australia, 1991, available for reference or purchase in the State Library.

ABORIGINAL PEOPLE OF SOUTH AUSTRALIA

The Mortlock Library of South Australiana holds a wide cross section of information about South Australia and its people, some of which relates to Aboriginal people.

Aboriginal people are the best source for Aboriginal family history. Families, friends and communities are invaluable sources of information. Approaching Aboriginal organisations is also a useful way to start.

Information relating to Aboriginal people can be found in the Mortlock Library but few sources of specific genealogical interest are held. Some of the sources held in the Mortlock Library are:

Reference material

In 1990, the Mortlock Library produced a ready reference guide to published material relating to Aboriginal people and received in the State Library of South Australia from 1951 to 1980.

* Mortlock Library of South Australiana. *Guide to publications held in the Mortlock Library of South Australiana relating to Aboriginal people.* Compiled by Bruce Hammond. Adelaide : Mortlock Library of South Australiana, 1990.

Private archives

These records have been donated from private sources. Examples are society records such as those of the Aborigines' Friends' Association and the Aborigines Advancement League.

* Mortlock Library of South Australiana. *Guide to archival records held in the Mortlock Library of South Australiana relating to Aboriginal people.* Compiled by David Jury. Adelaide : The Library, 1989. [i.e. 1990]. Provides a summary of useful sources.

Newspaper collection

The Mortlock Library holds newspapers dating from 1836. Many of these contain stories and reported incidents regarding Aboriginal people. A copy of the Department of Environment and Planning, Aboriginal Heritage Branch's index for newspapers is available in the Mortlock Library. This makes information in newspapers more readily accessible.

* *Newspaper index: references to Aborigines in Adelaide newspapers, 1836-1940.* Peggy Brock: project co-ordinator; Joy Chilman: editor; Tim Muecke: computer programmer. Adelaide : Aboriginal Heritage Branch, Department of Environment and Planning, 1989.

Other published sources

* State Library of South Australia. Family History Source Sheet no. 6. *Aboriginal family history.* Lists major published sources.

*Oral History Officer Beth Robertson instructing Julie Teddeo in the use of
the J.D. Somerville Oral History Collection's loan recording equipment.
Ms Teddeo interviewed her ninety-three year old grandmother Lucia Teddeo
[bottom photograph] about migrating, with her two sons, from the Abruzzi
region of Italy to join her husband in the Adelaide Hills in 1934. (OH 237)*

J. D. SOMERVILLE ORAL HISTORY COLLECTION

The J.D. Somerville Oral History Collection is a special collection within the Mortlock Library for oral history and related sound recordings (i.e. speeches, meetings, radio broadcasts). It is staffed by the Mortlock Library's Oral History Officer. The collection consists mainly of cassette tape recorded interviews and typewritten transcripts donated by the public. The Oral History Officer also conducts interviews and commissions interviews for special projects (such as oral histories of the Adelaide Gaol, the Goodwood Orphanage and women's political activities in South Australia).

Services available:

The Oral History Collection, which by 1994 amounted to over 2,000 interviews, has interviewee and subject indexes, as well as descriptions of each project or interview in the collection. The indexes are shelved at the reference desk of the Mortlock Library and tapes and transcripts are used by the public in the Historical Treasures Reading Room. The collection is available during State Library opening hours. Consultation with the Oral History Officer is by appointment (telephone (08) 207 7349).

The Oral History Officer offers Introductory Oral History Workshops several times a year for people interested in undertaking oral history interviewing themselves and also provides advice and assistance to interviewers and projects on an individual basis.

By using the Somerville Collection, or conducting their own interviews, family historians can gain invaluable information about the character, attitudes and activities of family members, both still living or living through the memories of others. By using a tape recorder – not just a pen and paper – to record information, family historians create a medium through which generations yet unborn will be able to hear the voices of today recounting their memories of the past.

PICTORIAL COLLECTION

This fascinating and growing collection includes more than 70,000 photographs of the people, places and activities in South Australia, from early days to the present. Some early photographs are also held for the Northern Territory (see page 54).

Women workers processing tobacco leaf near Penola (c.1932).
SSL:M:B12381

Arrangement

The photographs are arranged in different categories.

Localities collection: pictures of places, such as Burra, Murray River, Unley.

Portrait collection: photographs of people arranged alphabetically by surname.

General collection: pictures that do not fit into any specific category.

City Acres: photographs of buildings and street scenes of Adelaide arranged according to their City Acre number. A 'City Acre map' is held at the Mortlock Library reference desk and in the Historical Treasures Reading Room.

Adelaide Views: general panoramic views of Adelaide and specific places or items within the parkland area of Adelaide, such as the Botanic Gardens, University of Adelaide, Burns Statue, Railway Station.

Albums: photograph albums and thematic collections arranged under topics such as Costume or Ships.

Videodisk

The localities, portrait, and general collections, city acres, Adelaide views, and a small selection from the albums, can be viewed using videodisk technology sited in the Historical Treasures Reading Room. The system will quickly search for, and display, photographs that match descriptive words typed in by the user. It can also search in specified time frames, under familial names, district names, photograph reference numbers, and photographer's name.

An attached printer will supply a reference quality print for a small fee. Larger, high quality prints can be ordered from the State Library's Image Centre (see page viii).

The 54,000 photographs on videodisk are indexed in a descriptive subject index which is a useful starting point for finding pictures on a particular topic. This index also covers the albums that are not on the videodisk.

Each photograph has a number which is preceded by the letter 'B' – for example 'B48786'. As long as you note that number correctly, we should always be able to find that picture again.

In addition to 'B' numbers you may also find the following symbols in the Pictorial Index. These should be noted correctly as they serve to identify the categories in which photographs are housed:

Alb	identifies the	albums collection
Cos		costume collection
Gen		general collection
Loc		localities collection
Port		portraits collection
Ships		ships collection

Open access collection

Photographs that have been added to the pictorial collection since the conclusion of the videodisk project are available in the Historical Treasures Reading Room as the Open Access Collection. By using the printed subject or location indexes photographs can easily be found.

RARE BOOKS AND NAMED COLLECTIONS

Location:	State Library of South Australia North Terrace Adelaide 5000
Postal Address:	GPO Box 419 Adelaide 5001
Telephone:	(08) 207 7261
Hours:	Monday, Wednesday, Friday 1.30 pm to 5.00 pm Tuesday, Thursday 9.30 am to 5.00 pm Closed on public holidays

Rare Books and Named Collections contains manuscripts, books published anywhere in the world before 1801, Australian books published before 1901, rare, beautiful and valuable books published up to the present day, and any other predominantly non-South Australian material which needs to be read in a supervised area. This includes collections of mainly non-South Australian photographs, and some anthropological archival material.

FAMILY HISTORY SOURCES

Reference material

Some colonial Australian directories, alumni lists for Oxford and Cambridge Universities, some early editions of works on genealogy and heraldry, and rare or restricted works in the field of Australian anthropology are held. These works are all listed in the Bray Reference Library catalogues.

The most useful of these for people doing Australian Aboriginal family history is:

- Tindale, Norman. *Aboriginal tribes of Australia*. Berkeley : University of California Press, 1974. Contains maps showing the distribution of family groups and an extensive bibliography organised under family group names.

Pictorial collections

Shipping

The major sources for genealogists in Rare Books and Named Collections are the collections of shipping photographs and related information.

- *A.D. Edwardes Collection* contains about 8,000 photographs of ships, mainly sailing ships; the photographs were taken between the 1870s and the 1920s. Many, but not all, of the ships visited Australia, and the photographs were not necessarily taken in Australian waters.

- *A.L. Arbon – R.R. Le Maistre Collection* contains about 80,000 photographs of ships, and complements the Edwardes Collection because it mainly records twentieth century ships. It includes many photographs of the migrant ships of the 1940s and 1950s.

- *H.A. Godson Collection of River Murray Shipping* contains photographs on the history and ships of the River Murray. The only index to it at present is of the river craft, but it also contains local views and photographs of people.

It must be remembered that shipping photography was not commonly practised until the mid-1870s, and we are rarely able to help with photographs of ships which came to Australia before then. However, we have an extensive index to illustrations of ships in general reference works, including those held in other areas of the library, and this provides a lead to line drawings and paintings. The *Paul McGuire Maritime Library*, which is a discrete library within the general reference library, contains much shipping information.

Australian Aboriginal family history:

- *Mountford-Sheard Collection* contains a very large collection of photographs, some of which are cleared for general viewing, including pictures of identified individuals from the Flinders Ranges area.

SERVICES AVAILABLE

Staff are happy to assist with the use of reference materials, and to photocopy from some approved items, although photocopying of rare material is not generally permitted. A photographic print service is available subject to copyright and other considerations.

ROYAL GEOGRAPHICAL SOCIETY OF AUSTRALASIA
(SOUTH AUSTRALIAN BRANCH) INC.

Location:	State Library of South Australia North Terrace Adelaide 5000
Postal Address:	GPO Box 419 Adelaide 5001
Telephone:	(08) 207 7266 (08) 207 7265 (answer-phone for messages)
Hours:	Monday 1.30 pm to 5.00 pm Tuesday and Thursday 9.30 am to 5.00 pm Closed on public holidays

The society's library is a combination of three private collections, with the addition of later material. The largest of these private collections, the York Gate Library, was purchased by the society in 1905. It had been built up by S.W. Silver, a London merchant, and its collection of books, maps and periodicals relates particularly to voyages of exploration. It includes explorers' accounts, rare atlases, colonial histories and handbooks, and some genealogical 'treasures' relating to Great Britain, some of which date back to the 17th century.

In 1924 the society purchased the library of Thomas Gill, which is rich in Australiana, and contains early post office directories, almanacs, gazetteers, nomenclatures, and much biographical and historical information. Dr. F. Lucas Benham bequeathed part of his library, containing valuable anthropological and historical material, to the society in 1936. There is also the map collection, which includes early road maps, pastoral plans and cadastral maps.

The library is strong in local history material, and in 1990 Jim Faull donated his personal collection of 100 titles on South Australian local history, to which additions are made. The *Proceedings* of the society (now called the *South Australian Geographical Journal*) have been published since 1885 and are indexed. They are valuable for providing regional information, and sometimes local identities are mentioned in the articles. The general periodical collection also contains the newsletters and journals of local and interstate historical societies.

The society also holds over 200 manuscript items, principally concerned with the history of exploration and land settlement in Australia, and about 2,000 photographs.

SERVICES AVAILABLE:

The society's library is open to the general public and we welcome enquiries. There is a reading room and the librarian can provide assistance. Borrowing rights are limited to members of the society.

A brochure listing sources for genealogy held in the collection provides an easy guide to the material and is available for 50 cents:

- *Sources for genealogy held in the library of the Royal Geographical Society of Australasia (South Australian Branch) Inc.* Compiled by Roslyn Blandy. Adelaide : The Society, 1987.

PART 4

OTHER ORGANISATIONS HOLDING

FAMILY HISTORY SOURCES

INTRODUCTION

This section might prove useful for widening your research. It begins with a select listing of South Australian government and non-government organisations. This information was obtained from each organisation and was correct at March 1994. Most organisations listed are closed on public holidays.

The second section provides details of major interstate and overseas agencies.

SOUTH AUSTRALIAN

ADELAIDE CATHOLIC ARCHIVES

Location: 1st Floor
39 Wakefield Street
Adelaide 5000

Phone: (08) 210 8115

Hours: Monday to Thursday 9.00 am to 4.30 pm
Friday closed

The archives holds records which have been deposited over the years relating to the Catholic Church in South Australia.

The holdings include:

- Papers relating to the administration of the diocese from 1844 until the present time; however access to records less than 50 years old is restricted.
- Annual Australian Catholic directories (1881–). These can prove invaluable for locating priests, parishes and Catholic schools.
- Small collection of letters and diaries of the early priests from 1845.
- Papers from numerous Catholic societies (many now defunct) e.g. Catholic Young Men's Society, Catholic Guild for Social Studies.
- Full set of *Southern Cross* newspapers and some earlier Catholic newspapers.
- Various published parish histories and school histories.
- Photographs.
- Pre-1900 baptismal, marriage, burial and confirmation registers on microfiche. The microfiche are also available for consultation at the South Australian Genealogy and Heraldry Society Library (see page 77).

Services available:

Research must be done on the premises. Appointments are not essential, although it is wise to telephone beforehand to ascertain that assistance will be available. Copying facilities are available, however, original material may not be photocopied. Family history researchers are required to pay a fee for use of the library and facilities. For those unable to visit the library a correspondence research fee is charged per family name researched and per hour thereafter.

ADELAIDE CITY ARCHIVES

Location:	Topham Mall	Corporation of the City of Adelaide
	off Currie and Waymouth Streets	GPO Box 2252
	Adelaide 5000	Adelaide 5001
		Attn: Reference Services Archivist
Phone:	(08) 203 7439	Fax: (08) 203 7575
Hours:	Monday to Friday 9.00 am to 5.00 pm	

The Adelaide City Archives holds material relating to the activities of the Council and the Corporation of the City of Adelaide. Materials held date back to 1840 when the first Adelaide Corporation was formed and include written documents, maps, drawings, plans and photographs, as well as assessment records.

Services available:

Members of the public may visit the archives or make contact by telephone or in writing. There is no comprehensive index or catalogue to enable unaided research. The Reference Services Archivist will however, assist researchers with use of finding aids and identification of relevant records. Research is not undertaken by the archivist. Copying can be arranged.

ARCHIVES AND RESEARCH CENTRE, LUTHERAN CHURCH OF AUSTRALIA

Location:	101 Archer Street	
	North Adelaide 5006	
Phone:	(08) 267 1737	
Hours:	Monday, Tuesday, Thursday, Friday 9.30 am to 12.30 pm; 1.00 pm to 4.30 pm	

The centre is the official records depository for the Lutheran Church throughout Australia and has records spanning almost 150 years. However lodgement of parish records is voluntary not obligatory. Nevertheless, a solid nucleus of material has been built up, concentrating on the most populous and strategic Lutheran communities (principally of German and Scandinavian origin).

The holdings include:

- Official histories of the Church.
- Congregational histories.
- A large collection of family histories.
- Parish newspapers.
- Church registers for Adelaide and country areas (registers are also held for Victoria, Queensland, the Riverina district of New South Wales, and Western Australia).
- A large collection of Bibles and hymn books and artefacts from missions and parishes.
- Photographic collection of over 20,000 photographs.

Services available:

Family history researchers are required to pay a search fee per person per day. It is advisable to make enquiries or appointments before visiting to ensure that the wanted records are available. For those unable to visit the Centre, an hourly correspondence research fee is charged. Finding aids are available including, at this stage limited computer searches, for which a fee is charged plus a fee per page of printout.

AUSTRALIAN ARCHIVES, SOUTH AUSTRALIAN REGIONAL OFFICE

Location: 11-13 Derlanger Avenue   PO Box 119
           Collinswood 5081   Walkerville 5081

Phone: (08) 269 0100   Fax: (08) 269 3234

Hours: Monday to Friday 9.00 am to 12.30 pm; 1.30 pm to 4.30 pm

The Australian Archives, South Australian Regional Office is responsible for preserving the records of Commonwealth departments and authorities based in South Australia from 1901, as well as records from 1852 onwards of Colonial and State functions transferred to Federal administration.

Family history sources held:

- Ships' crews: registers of discharges (1853-1922), register of deserters (1852-1906) and some crew lists from 1907.
- SA lighthouse records (including logbooks) from the 1850s.
- Naturalization records (on microfilm) including certificates for:
    - South Australia   1848-1903
    - Victoria   1847-1903
    - Commonwealth   1904-1937
- An index of Commonwealth naturalizations subsequent to 1937 is also available. This allows reference to certificates located at Australian Archives, ACT Regional Office, PO Box 447, Belconnen, ACT 2617.
- Records of migration and immigration, particularly post-World War II including passenger lists from the 1940s (and some on microfilm for Melbourne, Newcastle and Queensland), migrant selection documents and alien registration records.
- Records of South Australian army enlistments from World War I and World War II (army pay files) and a few series dealing with Colonial defence and the Boer War (including microfilm of enlistees from other states).
- Records of internment of aliens during World War I and World War II, mostly at Loveday and also at Torrens Island.
- Commonwealth electoral rolls from 1904.

Services available:

Members of the public are expected to carry out their own research. Archives staff are available to give advice on search methods, the availability of records and the use of finding aids. Copies of records may be obtained on payment of a fee. The search room has microfilm reader-printer equipment for public use.

AUSTRALIAN ELECTORAL COMMISSION

Location: 5th Floor West
Commonwealth Centre
55 Currie Street
Adelaide 5000

GPO Box 344
Adelaide 5001

Phone: (08) 237 6555

Hours: Monday to Friday 8.30 am to 4.45 pm
During Federal elections there may be limited access to historical records

The Australian Electoral Commission holds South Australian Commonwealth electoral rolls from 1905. Only current electoral rolls on microfiche are held for all other states, the Northern Territory and the Australian Capital Territory.

Services available:

Members of the public requiring information from the records are expected to search the rolls on their own behalf. No public facility for copying records is available.

BANK SA LIBRARY

Formerly State Bank of South Australia

Location: 2nd Floor
97 King William Street
Adelaide 5000

GPO Box 399
Adelaide 5001

Phone: (08) 210 4348
(08) 210 4691

Fax: (08) 210 5417

Hours: The library is only open for public access on Wednesday 9.00 am to 12.00 noon

The Bank SA Library maintains an archival collection dating back to the establishment of the Savings Bank of South Australia in 1848. Early records of deposits, withdrawals, home loans, clubs and societies are available for public access by historical researchers on Wednesday mornings. The records are useful for genealogical research and for social, economic and architectural research.

Services available:

Telephone or fax enquiries will be accepted during normal working hours: Monday to Friday 8.30 am to 5.00 pm. The library is only open to visitors on Wednesday mornings.

BIRTHS, DEATHS AND MARRIAGES PRINCIPAL REGISTRY OFFICE

Location: Department of Consumer and
Business Affairs
Births, Deaths and Marriages
Registration Office
Edmund Wright House
59 King William Street
Adelaide 5000

GPO Box 1351
Adelaide 5001

Phone: (08) 226 8584

Hours: Monday to Friday 9.00 am to 4.30 pm

Since July 1842, law has required the registration of all births, deaths and marriages in South Australia. While it is true that the majority have been registered, it is also a fact that many events were not recorded or were recorded incorrectly. The Adelaide records only relate to events which occurred in South Australia.

Indexes are available for various periods between 1842–1916. Copies of these indexes are held on microfiche in the State Library Family History Collection and at other agencies.

The most useful details to be found on certificates are:
*   Births before July 1907: date of birth / name / sex / father and mother's names / residence (from May 1850 – Dec. 1874) / informant
*   Deaths before 1908: date of death / full name / sex / age / profession / usual residence / cause / place of death / informant [residence and place of death are not shown for the period 1842 – June 1856]
*   Marriages between 1842 – 24 August 1856: no. / when / where / names / ages / rank / signature and description / name of clergyman when registered / signature of clergyman / witnesses
*   Marriages between 25 August 1856 – 1867: when / full names / ages / condition / trade / residences / father's names / place / witnesses [condition e.g. bachelor, spinster]

Services available:
For those people unable to visit the office, and who wish to write for certificates, the following search details are required:
*   Birth: full name, specific date or year of birth, place of birth, and parents' names (mother's maiden name).
*   Death: full name, specific date or year of death, and usual residence, age.
*   Marriage: names of both people, specific date or year of marriage and place.
The office will advise people of the cost of obtaining a certified copy or extract of the certificate.

CHELTENHAM CEMETERY

See entry for Enfield Memorial Park

CHURCHES OF CHRIST IN SA INC.

Location: Conference Centre
263 Melbourne Street
North Adelaide

Phone: (08) 239 0233; (08) 276 5353 (home)

Hours: Strictly by appointment

Archivist: Mr. David G. Whyatt

The Churches of Christ were founded in South Australia in 1845. Only certain types of records are in existence because of the practices of the Church.

The holdings include:

- Congregational minutes which give some names of adult members received into the Church [i.e. the equivalent of baptism; there are no 'christening' records].
- Membership rolls [from which deaths can sometimes be gleaned].
- Marriage records [there are very few of these, as the Church only began keeping these with the introduction of the *Marriage Act* of 1961].
- Church publications, including official histories.

Services available:
Material can be made available at the front office by arrangement.

DEPARTMENT OF ENVIRONMENT AND NATURAL RESOURCES

Lands Titles Office

The conditions under which land has been 'held' in South Australia have seen a number of changes since 1836. The conditions have developed from the time when all land was held under lease from the Crown through to the introduction of both the *Real Property Act* and the Torrens System, which records the separation, or alienation of Crown land into private ownership, and any subsequent transactions. Therefore, before beginning a land search, enquirers need to determine by consulting a cadastral map, certificates of title, or any other property records within the family, the following details about the particular land holding:
- between which dates it was held
- whether under lease or freehold tenure
- county and hundred location

To assist further the Mortlock Reference desk holds leaflets entitled *Searching property records* and *Historic searching*, issued by DENR, as well as texts which explain the nineteenth century land legislation and systems.

All enquiries should then begin at the Lands Titles Office.

Lands Titles Office

Location: Colonel Light Centre   GPO Box 1354
                   25 Pirie Street   Adelaide   5001
                   Adelaide   5000

Phone: (08) 226 3983   Fax: (08) 226 3939

Hours: For ground floor computer enquiries regarding land ownership
                  Monday to Friday 9.30 am to 4.30 pm

                  For lodging and searching of titles: Monday to Friday 10.00 am to 4.00 pm

Certificates of title, issued from 1858, are held by the Lands Titles Office. When searching the history of a particular parcel of land, after having completed the Old System Section search, it is possible to follow the title forward to the current record or work back from the current title to the original titles.

When investigating a person's land transactions, the alphabetical index of property transactions from 1858 to the present should be consulted. This index is situated on the First floor of the Colonel Light Centre. Transactions for the period 1858-1975 are stored on microfilm, and transactions effected after 1975 are recorded on the LOTS computer file.

Services available:

Members of the public are expected to carry out their own research or engage a professional title searcher or conveyancer to search records on their behalf. Advice will be given by staff regarding the availability of records. Information about obtaining copies is also provided.

Old System Section (also known as the General Registry Office)

Location: 33 Carrington Street   GPO Box 1354
                   Adelaide   5000   Adelaide   5001

Phone: (08) 410 5061

Hours: Monday to Friday 9.30 am to 4.30 pm

The Old System Section (General Registry Office) holds records relating to freehold land transactions prior to the commencement of the *Real Property Act* of 1858. When searching the history of a particular parcel of land, it is necessary to begin by referring to the property books located on the First floor, Colonel Light Centre, 25 Pirie Street, Adelaide, for an application reference. Access to the original records may be restricted. Enquiries should then be made at the Old System Section (General Registry Office) where alphabetical indexes and other relevant documents are available.

When searching for the land transaction by a particular person, the Memorial Index and the Deposit Index at the Old System Section (General Registry Office) should be consulted.

DEPARTMENT OF STATE ABORIGINAL AFFAIRS
Culture and Site Services Branch

Location: 1st Floor
Centrepoint Building
22 Pulteney Street
Adelaide 5000

Phone: (08) 226 8900   Fax: (08) 226 8999

Hours: Strictly by appointment

The Culture and Site Services Branch holds references to newspapers, printed works and photographs. The photographic collection index and the newspaper card index have been transferred onto computer.

It is intended that these indexes will eventually be available through the Mortlock Library.

The Branch also maintains a reprint file of articles concerned with archaeology, anthropology and Aboriginal culture.

Services available:
Access to some of the records is restricted. Permission should be sought through the manager of the Culture and Site Services Branch.

It is recommended that you telephone the Branch for an appointment or for advice regarding material held before visiting.

ENFIELD MEMORIAL PARK

Location: Enfield Memorial Park
Browning Street   PO Box 294
Clearview 5085   Blair Athol 5084

Cheltenham Cemetery
Port Road
Cheltenham 5014

Phone: (08) 262 1321

Hours: Enfield Memorial Park office: Monday to Friday 9.00 am to 4.00 pm
There is pedestrian access to both cemeteries 7 days a week

Family History Sources
All records are held at Enfield Memorial Park. Enfield records date from 1947 onwards. Cheltenham records date from 1876 onwards. Enfield Memorial Park is the only major cemetery that has not been transcribed by the South Australian Genealogy and Heraldry Society.

Services available:

There is no public access to the records. Personal and/or written enquiries may be made. Fees may be applicable.

FLINDERS UNIVERSITY OF SOUTH AUSTRALIA

Location: Central Library
Sturt Road
Bedford Park 5042

Phone: (08) 201 2131

Hours: Telephone (08) 201 2131 to enquire about opening hours

Flinders University Central Library holds, as part of its historical research collection, some items which are of interest to genealogical researchers, including :

* Archives Authority of NSW. *Genealogical research kit.* (Microfilm)
* *Australian Joint Copying Project.* (Microfilm)
* *Tasmanian pioneers index.* 1803-1899. (Computer database)
* *Irish transportation records.* (Computer database)

Services available:

These materials are available for use by the general public, but no services are provided. Postal enquiries are not accepted.

GENEALOGICAL SOCIETY OF UTAH
(Church of Jesus Christ of Latter-Day Saints)

Adelaide Marion Family History Centre

Location: Cutting Road
Marion 5043

Phone: (08) 276 7849

Hours: Monday to Friday 12.00 to 4.00 pm
Closed on weekends
By special arrangement, the Centre can open on Saturday afternoons

Adelaide Modbury Family History Centre

Location: Von Braun Crescent
Modbury North 5092

Phone: (08) 263 1995

Hours: Tuesday 12.30 pm to 4.30 pm, 6.30 pm to 9.30 pm
Wednesday 6.30 pm to 9.30 pm
Thursday 12.30 pm to 4.30 pm
Friday 10.00 am to 4.00 pm, 6.30 pm to 9.30 pm

The society has branch libraries throughout Australia. The headquarters are located in Salt Lake City, Utah, United States of America.

The following branches can also be contacted by telephone:

Alice Springs	(089) 525 871	Port Pirie	(086) 321 964
Darwin	(089) 851 980	Swan Hill	(050) 322 086
Mildura	(050) 233 576	Whyalla	(086) 457 647
Mount Gambier	(087) 251 613		

The society has collected microfilm copies of a great many genealogical sources both from Australia and overseas. The Microfilm Ordering Centre for Australia is in Sydney where approximately one million microfilms are kept. Various indexes to the sources are available. The society's resources would be of particular benefit to those people wishing to pursue overseas sources for details about individuals prior to their arrival in South Australia. The St. Catherine's Indexes to births, deaths and marriages 1837–1904 are also held. Sources include the *International Genealogical Index* on computer as well as microfiche, and the 1891 English and Welsh census on microfiche.

Services available:

Researchers are not charged for use of the indexes. However a four week loan of the microfilm, obtained by completing a 'Microfilm Request' application form, does incur a charge. Average waiting time until receipt of the microfilm is two months. The researcher is notified when the film arrives and an appointment is made for use of the film. Information about current charges and costs of available copying facilities may be obtained from the Family History Centres.

LANDS DEPARTMENT

See Department of Environment and Natural Resources

PIONEERS ASSOCIATION OF SOUTH AUSTRALIA

> Location: 1st Floor
> Aston House
> 13 Leigh Street
> Adelaide 5000
>
> Phone: (08) 231 5055
>
> Hours: Thursday 10.00 am to 4.00 pm

The association holds records, portraits, and historical materials associated with pioneer settlement. Membership is restricted to those who have descended from a pioneer ancestor who arrived in South Australia by ship or other means on or before 31 December 1845. There is a list of members that includes the ships on which their ancestors arrived, and their dates of arrival.

Services available:

The association does not undertake detailed research.

PROBATE REGISTRY

Location: Ground Floor   301 King William Street
Supreme Court Building   Adelaide 5000
Corner Gouger and King William Streets
Adelaide 5000

Phone: (08) 204 0505 or (08) 204 0506

Hours: Monday to Friday 10.00 am to 4.00 pm

The Probate Registry holds wills and related documents from 1844. Only indexes covering 1844 to the present are available on open access and provide full name, place of residence and reference number of the will.

Services available:

Members of the public are expected to conduct their own research. However, correspondence from the country, interstate and overseas is accepted. Information regarding obtaining a copy of a deceased person's will and/or codicils which were proved in the Supreme Court of South Australia, and a copy of the corresponding grant of representation is available from the Registry staff.

RIVERLAND FAMILY HISTORY GROUP

Location: c/- PO Box 234
Loxton 5333

Phone: President: Mrs D. Thurmer (085) 821 796
Librarian: Mrs M. Bollenhagen (085) 838 217

Hours: Meetings are held on the first Wednesday of each month (except January and February) at 7.00 pm at the Church of Christ Hall, corner of McIntosh and Coneybeer Streets, Berri

SOUTH AUSTRALIAN GENEALOGY AND HERALDRY SOCIETY INC.

Location: Library   GPO Box 592
201 Unley Road   Adelaide 5001
Unley 5061

Phone: (08) 272 4222   Fax: (08) 272 4910

Hours: Tuesday 10.30 am to 2.30 pm
Tuesday (2nd and 4th weeks) 7.00 pm to 9.30 pm
Wednesday (2nd and 4th weeks) 10.30 am to 2.30 pm
Thursday 10.30 am to 2.30 pm
Saturday 10.30 am to 4.30 pm
Sunday (2nd and 4th weeks) 1.00 pm to 4.30 pm

The society library contains an extensive collection of genealogical, local history and related material.

The holdings include:

- Card, microfiche and microfilm records.
- Indexes to local, interstate and overseas records e.g. St. Catherine's Indexes to births, deaths and marriages 1837-1915.
- specialised indexes, e.g.
  Cemetery Index – index of gravestone inscriptions for most of the state's cemeteries, including details from a large number of cemetery burial registers.
  Blair index – index to birth, death and marriage notices from certain South Australian newspapers for selected periods.
  Adelaide Hospital and Destitute Asylum indexes – indexes to people admitted to the respective institutions; sometimes useful in identifying the ship of arrival. [These are also available at State Records which holds the original records.].
  Index to Register of deserters – index to records held at the Australian Archives, South Australian Regional Office for the period 1852-1940.

Services available:

The society offers research services at a nominal fee to members and the general public who are unable to use the society library. Research is restricted to matters of a specific nature. General or extensive research is not undertaken. Membership fees are charged at ordinary, associate, concession and affiliate rates.

Country branches have been established in the Yorke Peninsula and Riverland areas. (See Yorke Peninsula Family History Group, and Riverland Family History Group.)

SOUTH AUSTRALIAN MARITIME MUSEUM

Location:	126 Lipson Street Port Adelaide 5015	119 Lipson Street Port Adelaide 5015
Phone:	(08) 240 0200	Fax: (08) 341 2208
Hours:	Normal hours are Tuesday to Sunday 10.00 am to 5.00 pm During school holidays and on public holidays (except for Christmas Day) the museum is also open on Monday	

The museum, opened in December 1986, has a variety of exhibits and displays relating to South Australian maritime matters. A single admission charge covers entrance to the Lipson Street galleries, two historic vessels and Port Adelaide Lighthouse.

Family History sources:

A unique feature of the museum is its computer database of migrant passenger arrivals for the periods 1836-1885 and 1925-1956, which is available for public use. The first period is based on information compiled for the *Biographical index of South Australians 1836-1885*. The second period is based on passenger lists held at the Mortlock Library (to 1940) and at the Australian Archives, South Australian Regional Office (from 1940s). The second period of the database is of particular benefit to family historians in that a consolidated passenger index has been created to these records. Information given includes: surname and given name or initials, age at arrival, ship, year and occupation. A copy of this index is also available in hardcopy and on microfiche in the State Library Family History Collection (see page 36).

Services available:
Printouts from the database are available at cost.
For postal, fax and telephone enquiries, a search fee plus printout fee is charged.

SOUTH AUSTRALIAN MUSEUM
Division of Anthropology; Aboriginal Family History Project

Location:	North Terrace
	Adelaide 5000

Phone:	(086) 345 362 Doreen Kartinyeri	Fax:	(086) 345 362
	(08) 207 7410 Neva Wilson		(08) 207 7390
	(08) 207 7409 Barry Craig		(08) 207 7390

Hours: Museum staff are available to help find the information you may be looking for, but it is easier for staff if you write or telephone first to make an appointment. You can ring to make an appointment between 9.00 am and 5.00 pm, Monday to Friday

The museum holds an extensive collection of Aboriginal genealogical information and named photographs, most of which was recorded by Norman Tindale.

From 1928-1957, Norman Tindale and colleagues at the South Australian Museum visited Aboriginal people on missions and government stations throughout Australia. Records for many of the localities he visited include photographs and detailed genealogies.

Localities visited in South Australia were:
Bookabie, Colona, Erliwanjawanja, Ernabella, Koonibba, Mirramitta, Nepabunna, Nullarbor Station, Ooldea, Pandi Pandi, Point McLeay, Point Pearce, Poka, Poka Gap, Port Augusta, Swan Reach and Umbukulu.

A full list of localities visited in each state is provided in the brochure *The Aboriginal Family History Project of the South Australian Museum* (copies of this brochure are also available at the Mortlock Library reference desk).

Aboriginal people from all over Australia are invited to use these resources, but it is easier for museum staff if you make an appointment before visiting.

Researchers who wish to use the collection on behalf of another individual, family or community, should first obtain written permission from those concerned.

Copying, microfilming, indexing and publication projects are expected to make the collection more accessible to Aboriginal people throughout Australia. For example, copies of genealogies and photographs relating to Queensland have been provided to the John Oxley Library, State Library of Queensland. Copies of Lake Tyers and Cummeragunja genealogies and photographs are located at the Museum of Victoria in Melbourne. Copies of Western Australian genealogies and photographs are located at the Aboriginal Affairs Planning Authority in Perth.

SOUTH EAST FAMILY HISTORY GROUP INC.

Location: (Old Church building) PO Box 758
14 Stuckey Street Millicent 5280
Millicent 5280

Hours: Library is open: Wednesdays 1.00 pm to 4.00 pm
Fourth Thursday each month (meeting night) 6.30 pm to 7.30 pm
First Saturday each month 1.00 pm to 5.00 pm

There are area representatives at: Millicent, Beachport, Rendelsham, Tantanoola, Mount Gambier, Moorak, Kingston, Naracoorte, Keith and Penola.

Use of the South East Family History Group Inc. library is free for members. There is a charge for use of microfiche per half hour. A charge is applicable for non-members to use the library.

Postal enquirers should enclose a stamped self-addressed envelope. A research fee is applicable with rates varying for members and non-members.

STATE BANK OF SOUTH AUSTRALIA LIBRARY

See Bank SA Library

STATE RECORDS

Formerly Public Record Office of South Australia and South Australian Archives

Location: Norwich Centre PO Box 713
55 King William Road North Adelaide 5006
North Adelaide 5006

Phone: (08) 267 8230 Fax: (08) 267 8227

Hours: Monday to Wednesday, Friday 9.30 am to 5.00 pm
Thursday 1.00 pm to 8.00 pm

State Records is responsible for selecting, preserving and providing access to records of archival significance created by state, local and semi-government agencies since European settlement in South Australia.

Family history sources held:

- Letters and other communications received and sent by the Colonial Secretary including correspondence with, or about, early settlers (1836-1856).
- Succession duty records (1875–).
- Social welfare records, including material about Children's homes and records of the Destitute Persons Department.
- Surrendered Crown Leases (1887-1927).
- Local Government rate assessment books.
- Applications of emigrant labourers for free passage (1836-1841).
- 1841 Census, including alphabetical index.
- Official passenger lists for assisted immigrants (1845-1886).
- Official lists of people departing from Port Adelaide for overseas ports (1911-1940).
- State electoral rolls (1884-1913).
- Gaol records of the Department of Correctional Services (1830s) e.g. Adelaide and Yatala prisoners' registers.
- Inquest depositions; Coroner's reports from the Police (1839–).
- Government hospital admission registers.
- Government school records e.g. admission registers.
- Government employment records e.g. Railways.

In most cases indexes are available to the records, and in some cases detailed finding aids are also available. Some indexes on microfiche are also available for purchase.

Services available:

- a duty archivist is in attendance to assist with reference enquiries and will be pleased to discuss research requirements at any time.
- specific enquiries may be made by telephone.
- country, interstate and overseas enquiries by correspondence are accepted. A fee applies for any research carried out by the archivists.
- advice on access, copyright, copying.
- photographic copying service.

As much further information of genealogical interest may be found in record series other than those listed above, researchers should also discuss with staff their particular areas of interest, besides consulting guides published by State Records, such as:

- *Ancestors in archives – A guide to family history sources in the official records of South Australia.*
- *Guide to records relating to women.*
- *Guide to records relating to Aboriginal people.*
- *Aboriginal resource kit.*
- *Guide to records relating to people of non-English speaking backgrounds.*

TELECOMMUNICATIONS MUSEUM COLLECTION

Location: Curator of Technology
c/- History Trust of South Australia
Institute Building
122 Kintore Avenue
Adelaide 5000

Phone: (08) 207 7565   Fax: (08) 207 7557

Hours: By appointment

Holdings include:
- Early South Australian and Northern Territory telephone directories.
- Personnel records of former employees of the SA Telegraphs Department, PMG Department and Telecom Australia.
- Historical information about telegraph, telephones and radio broadcasting services.
- Technical information.
- Photographs of equipment and installations.
- A reference service is available by mail, telephone or appointment.

WEST TERRACE CEMETERY
Department of Housing and Urban Development

Location: 161 West Terrace
Adelaide 5000

Phone: (08) 231 2062

Hours: Office: Monday to Friday 8.00 am to 4.00 pm
Closed 12.00 pm to 12.30 pm for lunch

Cemetery: Open every day 8.00 am to 5.30 pm for pedestrian traffic only

Records held date from 1840 to the present. For details of burials in the general section of the cemetery between 1910 and 1939, a year of death is required. The South Australian Genealogy and Heraldry Society has a set of West Terrace Cemetery records on microfiche.

Services available:
There is no public access to the records. All searches are made by staff only. When making postal enquiries please include stamps for return postage.

YORKE PENINSULA FAMILY HISTORY GROUP

Location: Research Librarian
Yorke Peninsula Family History Group
PO Box 260
Kadina 5554

Phone: (088) 212 704 (Northern Yorke Peninsula Library)

Hours: Tuesday 10.00 am to 12.00 pm
Thursday 2.00 pm to 4.00 pm

Meetings are held on the first Thursday of each month (except January) at 8.00 pm at the Northern Yorke Peninsula Library, Graves Street, Kadina. The Yorke Peninsula Family History Group Library (including birth, death and marriage district registers (see pages 102-108) for County Daly with indexes and certificates) is housed in the Northern Yorke Peninsula Library.

Services available:
Research enquiries may be directed to the Research Librarian. Please include a stamped, self-addressed envelope. Fees vary.

INTERSTATE

AUSTRALIAN CAPITAL TERRITORY

AIF Project

Department of History
University College
Australian Defence Force Academy
Canberra 2600

The AIF Project collects information on all those who served in the Australian Imperial Force (1914-1921) and makes it available to enquirers on a fee-for-service basis. Brochures are available from the State Library of SA Family History Collection or from the above address.

Australian War Memorial

Limestone Avenue
Campbell 2601
(06) 243 4312; (06) 243 4315

Manager, Information Services
Australian War Memorial
GPO Box 345
Canberra 2601

The Memorial is unable to undertake any research on your behalf. If you cannot visit personally, a list of individuals who undertake research on a commercial basis is available from the Memorial.

National Library of Australia

Parkes Place
Parkes 2600
(06) 262 1111

Registrar of Births, Deaths and Marriages

Corner Allara Street and Constitution Avenue
Canberra City 2601
(06) 207 0460

GPO Box 788
Canberra City 2601

NEW SOUTH WALES

Archives Office of New South Wales

City Search Room
2 Globe Street
The Rocks
Sydney 2000
(02)237 0254; (02) 237 011

Kingswood Search Room
O'Connell Street
Kingswood 2747
(02) 673 1788

All Archives Office of New South Wales correspondence should be sent to:

Research Services
Archives Office of NSW
2 Globe Street
The Rocks
Sydney 2000

Registry of Births, Deaths and Marriages

191 Thomas Street
Haymarket 2000
(02) 228 8988

Box 30
GPO Sydney 2001

State Library of New South Wales

Macquarie Street
Sydney 2000
(02) 230 1414

NORTHERN TERRITORY

Northern Territory Archives Service

10 McMinn Street.
Darwin 0800
(089) 89 5188

GPO Box 874
Darwin 0801

Registrar of Births, Deaths and Marriages

Corner Cavenagh and Bennett Streets
Darwin 0800
(089) 89 6119

GPO Box 3021
Darwin 0801

State Library of the Northern Territory

25 Cavenagh Street
Darwin 0800
(089) 89 7177

GPO Box 42
Darwin 0801

QUEENSLAND

Queensland State Archives

435 Compton Road
Runcorn 4113
(07) 875 8755

PO Box 1397
Sunnybank Hills 4109

Registrar-General of Births, Deaths and Marriages

33-35 Herschel Street
Brisbane 4000
(07) 227 5802

PO Box 188
Albert Street
Brisbane 4001

Only records from 1890 are available. For pre 1890 records contact the Queensland State Archives.

State Library of Queensland

Queensland Cultural Centre
Corner Stanley and Peel Streets
South Brisbane 4101
(07) 840 7666; (07) 840 7785

GPO Box 3488
South Brisbane 4101

TASMANIA

Archives Office of Tasmania

91 Murray Street
Hobart 7000
(002) 33 7490; (002) 33 7488

Registry of Births, Deaths and Marriages

15 Murray Street
Hobart 7000
(002) 33 3793

PO Box 198
Hobart 7001

For records after 1899 only. Pre 1899 records are widely available in microform (see page 41).

State Library of Tasmania

91 Murray Street
Hobart 7000
(002) 33 7458

VICTORIA

Public Record Office of Victoria

City Search Room
4th Floor
318 Little Bourke Street
Melbourne 3000
(03) 651 4131

Laverton Search Room
57 Cherry Lane
Laverton North 3026
(03) 360 9665

Registry of Births, Deaths and Marriages

295 Queen Street
Melbourne 3000
(03) 603 5900

GPO Box 4332
Melbourne 3001

State Library of Victoria

328 Swanston Street
Melbourne 3000
(03) 669 9888

WESTERN AUSTRALIA

Library and Information Service of WA

Alexander Library Building
Perth Cultural Centre
James Street
Perth 6000
(09) 427 3111

Registrar-General's Office

Level 10 Westralia Square
141 St. Georges Terrace
Perth 6000
(09) 264 1555

GPO Box 7720
Cloisters Square
Perth 6850

State Archives of Western Australia

Library and Information Services of WA
Alexander Library Building
Perth Cultural Centre
James Street
Perth 6000
(09) 427 3111

OVERSEAS

EIRE

Registrar General

8-11 Lombard Street East
Dublin 2
Eire

ENGLAND AND WALES

Office of Population Censuses and Surveys

General Register Office
Smedley Hydro
Southport
Merseyside
England PR8 2HH

Public Record Office

Chancery Lane
London
England WC2A 1LR
or
Ruskin Avenue
Kew
Richmond
Surrey
England TW9 4DU

NORTHERN IRELAND

General Register Office

Oxford House
49-55 Chichester Street
Belfast
Northern Ireland BT1 4HL

SCOTLAND

General Register Office for Scotland

New Register House
Edinburgh
Scotland EHI 3YT

PART 5
RESEARCH AGENTS, SOCIETIES
AND DISTRICT REGISTERS

GUIDE TO SOCIETIES AND RESEARCH AGENCIES

There are a number of societies and agencies that may undertake more extensive research relating to South Australian family history, for a fee. **It should be understood that the State Library accepts no responsibility for any arrangements made between a client and a researcher.** As the fees charged by different researchers may vary, you should find out the costs before commissioning any work.

- **Association of Professional Historians Inc.**
  Institute Building, 122 Kintore Avenue, Adelaide 5000

  The association, formed in 1981, is an independent professional body representing the interests of qualified people who are concerned with encouraging professional standards of historical research and writing. Professional historians undertake research, evaluate and assess information, prepare reports, manuscripts and publications. They are aware of the vast array of archival material and its location, and are skilled in many techniques including historical interpretation and oral history.

  The *Directory of consultant historians and researchers* lists members (with details of their expertise) who are available to undertake historical research work and to prepare projects for publication. Copies of the *Directory* can be obtained from the Mortlock Library, State Records or by writing to the secretary of the association.

- **Australasian Association of Genealogists and Record Agents**
  PO Box 268, Oakleigh 3166

  Founded in 1977, the association aims to offer the public the services of reliable and competent genealogists and record agents. Membership is only open to qualified persons of considerable practical experience in the fields of genealogy and record searching.

  Fees charged are based on the time spent and costs involved in handling the commission.

- **South Australian Genealogy and Heraldry Society Inc.**
  GPO Box 592, Adelaide 5001

  The society was formed in 1973 to assist persons interested in family history and related areas. The society offers research services at a nominal fee to members and the general public unable to use the society library. Research is restricted to matters of a specific nature and general or extensive research is not undertaken.

For listings of other agencies see the Adelaide Yellow Pages telephone book.
Headings to look for are:

> Genealogy
> Social and cultural research
> Title searchers (for land title searches)

SOUTH AUSTRALIAN HISTORICAL ORGANISATIONS

The following list was prepared by the State History Centre, Old Parliament House, Adelaide. Telephone (08) 207 1077. Information was current at March 1994.

Since 1982 the History Trust of South Australia has maintained a register of South Australian voluntary historical organisations and information agencies. In 1992 the register became the responsibility of the State History Centre, a division of the History Trust.

The contact file for National Trust branches is maintained by their head office. (Telephone (08) 223 1655). Their titles have been abbreviated in this list but each of them functions as a branch of the National Trust of South Australia.

Only museum groups with general memberships are included in this listing. A separate register of museums is maintained by the State History Centre's Museum Services Manager. (Telephone (08) 207 1075).

Aboriginal – see State
Adelaide Bus Preservation Group: c/- Mr C Mountain 51a Robsart Street Parkside 5063.
Adelaide Gaol Preservation Society: 18 Gaol Road Thebarton 5031. Mrs S Scheiffers
   Ph. (08) 231 4062
Adelaide Hills Motor Restorers Club: PO Box 65 Littlehampton 5250. Mr B Heath
   Ph. (08) 296 2899 (H)
Adelaide Historical Bottle Club: PO Box 344 Hindmarsh 5007. Mr R Billinger
   Ph. (08) 282 8704 (W), (08) 356 7689 (H)
Angaston (formation pending): 8 Sarah Street Angaston 5353. Dr B Gransbury
   Ph. (085) 64 2266 (W), (085) 64 3222 (H)
Anthropological Society of South Australia: c/- Mr P Clarke Anthropology Section
   SA Museum North Terrace Adelaide 5000. Ph. (08) 207 7500
Archivists – see Australian
Association of Professional Historians: Institute Building 122 Kintore Avenue Adelaide
   5000. Ms A Painter Ph. (08) 276 8986
Auburn National Trust: PO Box 16 Auburn 5451. Miss H Karger Ph. (088) 47 4096,
   (088) 49 2215 (AH)
Aurora Heritage Action: c/- 120 Wakefield Street Adelaide 5000. Mr J Stratmann
   Ph. (08) 390 1352
Australasian Maritime Historical Society (SA Branch): PO Box 89 Lobethal 5241.
   Mr R H Parsons Ph. (08) 389 4292
Australian Electric Transport Museum: GPO Box 2012 Adelaide 5001.
   Ph. (08) 210 4020 (W), (08) 258 9772 (H)
Australian & New Zealand History of Education Society (SA Branch):
   c/- Mrs L Trethewey Uni of South Australia (Magill Campus) 15 Lorne Avenue Magill
   5072. Mrs L Trethewey Ph. (08) 278 7491 (H)
Australian Railway Historical Society (SA Division): GPO Box 507 Adelaide 5001.
   Mr A Raphael Ph. (08) 236 3213 (W), (08) 379 0104 (H)

Australian Society of Archivists Inc (SA Branch): PO Box 8182
  Hindley Street Post Office Adelaide 5000. Ms B Bean Ph. (08) 349 5577
Australian Theatre Historical Society (SA Representative): c/- Ms P Breuninger
  37 Dorene Street St Marys 5042.
Aviation – see Civil, South Australian, West Beach
Balaklava National Trust: c/- 16 Harris Street Balaklava 5461. Miss J Zacher
  Ph. (088) 62 1467
Barmera National Trust: PO Box 318 Barmera 5345. Mrs B Gow Ph. (085) 88 2521
Barossa Goldfields Historical Society: c/- Mr R Swarbrick c/- PMB Cockatoo Valley 5351.
  Ph. (085) 24 4548
Barossa Light Horse Historical Association: c/- Mr C Lloyd PO Williamstown 5351.
  Ph. (08) 43 3307 (W), (085) 24 6405 (H)
Barossa Valley Archives & Historical Trust Inc.: c/- Pastor P Scherer PO Box 51 Tanunda
  5352. Ph. (085) 63 2337
Barossa Valley Machinery Preservation Society: c/- Mr K P Rohrlach 21 Dean Street
  Angaston 5353. Ph. (085) 63 3407 (W), (085) 64 2478 (H)
Beachport & District National Trust: PO Beachport 5280. Mr T Georgeson
  Ph. (087) 35 8147
Berri National Trust: PO Box 428 Berri 5343. Mr N Storry
Blanchetown Heritage Society: c/- D Zadow PMB 4 Blanchetown 5357.
  Ph. (085) 40 5021 (H)
Booleroo Steam & Traction Preservation Society Inc.: PO Box 7 Caltowie 5490.
  Mr C Becker Ph. (086) 65 5032
Bottles – see Adelaide
Brighton Historical Society: PO Box 544 Brighton 5048. Ms D Mills
  Ph. (08) 296 4946 (H)
Brinkworth History Group: c/- Mrs H Weckert PO Box 12 Brinkworth 5464.
  Ph. (088) 46 6086
Built Heritage Groups of SA: c/- Enfield and Districts Historical Society.
Burnside Historical Society: PO Box 152 Glenside 5065. Mr R House
  Ph. (08) 379 9015
Burra Historical Society: c/- Burra Community Library Burra 5417.
Burra National Trust: PO Box 97 Burra 5417. Mr J Hawker Ph. (088) 93 2270
Buses – see Adelaide
Campbelltown Historical Society Inc.: c/- Mrs C Nightingale 16 Rodney Avenue Tranmere
  5073.
Cape Horners Australia Inc.: c/- Mr J Hopton 63 Hurtle Square Adelaide 5000.
  Ph. (08) 232 1110 (H)
Carl Linger Memorial Committee Inc.: c/- Mr R Wallace 1/4 New Street Plympton 5038.
  Ph. (08) 293 6664
Cars – see Maitland, Northern, Sporting
Ceduna National Trust: c/- Box 583 Ceduna 5690. Mr A Lowe Ph. (086) 25 2711
Central Yorke Peninsula National Trust: PO Box 106 Maitland 5573.
  Miss B Newman Ph. (088) 32 2220
Civil Aviation Historical Society SA - NT Division: c/- Mr D Temby 23 Balham Avenue
  Kingswood 5062.

Clare & District National Trust: PO Box 251 Clare 5453. Mr J Haynes
Ph. (088) 42 2374

Clare Regional History Group: PO Box 6 Clare 5453. Secretary Ph. (088) 42 3817 (W),
(088) 42 2733 (H)

Cleve National Trust: PO Box 170 Cleve 5640. Mrs A Turnbull Ph. (086) 28 2038

Coober Pedy Historical Society: PO Box 216 Coober Pedy 5723.

Coomandook, Peake & Districts Historical Society: c/- Mrs T White PO Box 34 Cooke
Plains 5261. Ph. (085) 73 3031

Coromandel Valley & District National Trust: c/- 4 Baust Crescent Coromandel Valley 5051.
Mrs J McHenry Ph. (08) 278 7549

Crystal Brook History Group: c/- District Council Blowman Street Crystal Brook 5523.

Crystal Brook National Trust: PO Box 55 Crystal Brook 5523. Mrs J Sawyer
Ph. (086) 36 2396

Cummins Society: PO Box 507 Plympton 5038. Ms C Jennings Ph. (08) 297 2399 (W)

Dental – see South Australian

Department of Transport Northfield Depot Heritage Group: c/- Mr R Earle PO Box 82
Blair Athol 5084.

Dudley National Trust: PO Box 550 Penneshaw 5222.

East Torrens Historical Society: c/- Mrs J Chapman District Council of East Torrens
1 Crescent Drive Norton Summit 5136. Mrs J Chapman Ph. (08) 390 1832

Echunga & District Historical Society: c/- Mr J Jenneson Echunga 5153.
Ph. (08) 388 8114 (H)

Education – see Australian

Eighteen Thirty Six Royal Marines: c/- Mr B Reader 17 Waverley Drive Willunga 5172.
Ph. (085) 56 2878

Enfield & Districts Historical Society: PO Box 511 Prospect East 5082. Mrs J Hopkins
Ph. (08) 269 4644

Engineering Heritage Branch: The Institution of Engineers Australia (SA Division)
11 Bagot Street North Adelaide 5006. Mr D Kemp Ph. (08) 363 1000

Family History – see Port Pirie, Riverland, South Australian, South East, Southern Eyre, Yorke
Peninsula

Fire Services – see South Australian

Fleurieu Antique Rural Machinery Society: c/- Mr D Light 36 Corriedale Hill Drive Happy
Valley 5159. Ph. (08) 381 8064

Folk Federation of South Australia: GPO Box 525 Adelaide 5000. Mr K Preston
Ph. (08) 211 7899 (W), (08) 468 132 (H)

Fort Glanville Historical Association Inc: c/- Mr D Baker 5 Shalford Terrace Campbelltown
5074.

Franklin Harbor National Trust: PO Box 5 Cowell 5602. Mr A R Guthleben
Ph. (086) 29 2032

Friends of Kingston House: c/- Mrs B Hardy 6 Marine Parade Seacliff 5049.
Mrs B Hardy Ph. (08) 296 7348

Friends of Old Government House: c/- Mrs E Campbell 31 MacArthur Avenue Warradale
5046. Mrs E Campbell Ph. (08) 298 6432

Friends of The Oscar W Society Inc: PO Box 527 Goolwa 5214.

Friends of The Waite Historic Precinct: Waite Agricultural Research Institute
Glen Osmond 5064. Ms Y Routledge Ph. (08) 303 7425 (Mon-Thurs)

Gaol – see Adelaide

Gas – see South Australian

Gawler Machinery Restorers Club: c/- Mr D Beatty 10 Hemaford Grove Gawler East
5118. Ph. (085) 22 2198

Gawler National Trust: c/- G R Carse 40 Bella Street Gawler East 5118. Mrs G Carse
Ph. (085) 22 2548

Gawler Oral History Society: PO Box 152 Glenside 5065.

Genealogy – see Port Pirie, Riverland, South Australian, South East, Southern Eyre, Yorke
Peninsula

Georgetown Heritage Society: c/- Mrs H Fogarty PO Box 41 Georgetown 5472.
Ph. (086) 62 4123

German Descendants Group: c/- SA German Association Inc 223 Flinders Street Adelaide
5000. Mr Max Otto Ph. (08) 31 4028

Ghan Railway Preservation Society (SA) Inc.: c/- Mr S Coxon 23 McKenzie Street
Coromandel Valley 5051. Ph. (08) 260 3028

Glenelg National Trust: c/- Mr J Messenger 21 Maturin Road Glenelg 5045.
Ph. (08) 223 1468, (08) 294 3427

Glenside Hospital Historical Society: c/- Psychology Dept Glenside Hospital PO Box 17
Eastwood 5063. Ph. (08) 372 1158 (W), (08) 373 0730 (H)

Green Triangle Machinery Restorers Club: c/- 12 Amos Street Mount Gambier 5290.
Allan Adamson Ph. (087) 25 7885

Goolwa National Trust: PO Box 470 Goolwa 5214. Miss D Tuckwell Ph. (085) 55 1512

Gumeracha District Local History Centre: PO Box 126 Gumeracha 5233.

Hahndorf National Trust: c/- 35 English Street Hahndorf 5245. Miss L Davidge
Ph. (08) 388 7495

Hallett Local History Group: c/- Mrs J McDowell Hallett 5419.

Happy Valley National Trust: c/- Mr B Burton RMB 302A Pole Road Iron Bank 5153.
Ph. 267 3200, 388 2409 (AH)

Harefield Society Australia: c/- Mr B Watkins 19 Davenport Terrace Hilton 5033.

Henley & Grange Historical Society: PO Box 56 Henley Beach 5022. Ms K Barrett
Ph. (08) 353 1307

Heritage Arms Society Inc.: PO Box 552 Eastwood 5063.

Hindmarsh Historical Society: PO Box 22 Hindmarsh 5007. Ms J Urlwin
Ph. (08) 46 9871 (W), (08) 46 8035 (H)

Historians – see Association

Historical Society of South Australia Inc.: 122 Kintore Avenue Adelaide 5000. Dr R Nicol
Ph. (08) 297 9844 (H)

Historical Society of the Uniting Church in SA: c/- Dr A D Hunt 13 Alfreda Street
Brighton 5048.

Historical Society of Woodville: c/- Mr D A Hamilton PO Box 58 Woodville 5011.
Mr D Hamilton Ph. (08) 345 5716

History of Science, Ideas & Technology Group: 2A Thorngate Street Thorngate 5082.
Dr P Payne Ph. (08) 269 6879

History Teachers Association of South Australia: c/- SA Institute of Teachers
153a Greenhill Road Parkside 5063. Ms A Buxton Ph. (08) 379 4575

Horse – see Barossa, South Australian

Ideas – see History

Institution of Engineers – see Engineering

Institution of Surveyors, Australia (SA Division) Historical Subcommittee:
AMF Building Conyngham Street Glenside 5065.

Italian Historical Society: c/- Mr P Nocella 565 Lower North East Road Campbelltown 5074.
Ph. (08) 365 0377

Jamestown National Trust: PO Box 23 Jamestown 5491. Ph. (086) 64 1331

John McDouall Stuart Society: c/- Mr S W Marchant PO Box 398 Eastwood 5063.

Kadina National Trust: c/- 24 South Terrace Kadina 5554. Mr L Franks
Ph. (088) 21 1083

Kangaroo Island National Trust: PO 418 Kingscote 5223. Mr L Howard
Ph. (0848) 2 2308

Kangaroo Island Pioneers Association: c/- Mrs L Henderson 17 Olympus Avenue Modbury
Heights 5092. Ph. (08) 264 2763 (H)

Kapunda Historical Society: PO Box 332 Kapunda 5373. Ms J Jones
Ph. (085) 66 2902 (W), (085) 66 2657 (H)

Karoonda & District Historical Society: c/- Mr D Anderson Karoonda 5307.
Ph. (085) 78 1179

Keith National Trust: PO Box 428 Keith 5267. Mrs H Stanton Ph. (087) 55 1584

Kensington & Norwood Historical Society Inc: PO Box 3153 Norwood 5067.
Mrs Jean Wright Ph. (08) 332 5780

Kimba & Gawler Ranges Historical Society: c/- Mrs M Eatts PO Box 134 Kimba 5641.
Ph. (086) 27 7201

Kingston House – see Friends

Kingston National Trust: PO Box 93 Kingston(S-E) 5275. Mrs K White
Ph. (087) 67 2114

Kingston Senior Citizens Oral History Group: c/- Mr R J Smith 15 Cock Street
Kingston(S-E) 5275.

Koppio National Trust: c/- PMB 35 Port Lincoln 5607. Mrs C J Calderwood
Ph. (086) 84 4208

Labour History – see Society for the Study of

Lameroo District Historical Society: c/- District Clerk Lameroo 5302.
Ph. (085) 76 3002 (W), (085) 76 3088 (H)

Light Horse – see Barossa, South Australian

Lobethal Historical Society: c/- Mrs L E Miller PO Lobethal 5241. Ph. (08) 389 6413

Lock & District Historical Society: c/- Mrs J Shipard PO Box 48 Lock 5633.

Lower Murray National Trust: c/- Mr N Jaensch 'Pretoria' Tailem Bend 5260.
Ph. (085) 72 3670

Loxton District Historical Village Society: c/- Mr M Wedding 52 Kokoda Terrace Loxton
5333. Ph. (085) 84 7942

Loxton Public Library Local History Group: c/- Mrs K Weatherall Loxton Public Library
Loxton 5333.

Lucindale Historical Society: PO Box 187 Lucindale 5272. J Mugford Ph. (087) 66 0036

Lyndoch & District Historical Society: c/- Mr S A Hausler PO Box 6 Lyndoch 5351.
Ph. (085) 24 6071

Machinery – see Adelaide, Barossa, Booleroo, Fleurieu, Gawler, Green Triangle, History

Maitland Auto Preservation Society Inc.: c/- Mr B Landt 1 Elizabeth Street Maitland 5573.
Ph. (088) 32 2383

Mallala Historical Society: PO Mallala 5502.

Mannum Dock Museum Board: PO Mannum 5238. Mr R Bowring (085) 69 1206

Marion Historical Society: c/- Mr C Rankin 47 William Street South Plympton 5038.
Ph. (08) 297 8189

Maritime – see Australasian, Cape Horners, Friends, Port of, Society

Marree Historical Society: Sixth Street Marree 5733.

Melrose National Trust: PO Box 68 Melrose 5483. Mrs P Michael Ph. (086) 66 2070

Meningie Historical Society Inc.: Ms J Woolston PO Box 186 Meningie 5264.

Mid-Murraylands Local History Group: c/- Swan Reach Area School PO Box 31
Swan Reach 5253. Ms J Wilkinson Ph. (085) 70 2053

Milang & District Historical Society: c/- Milang High School PO Box 17 Port Elliot 5212.
Ms A Basham

Military – see Eighteen Thirty Six, Fort Glanville, Heritage Arms

Military Historical Society of Australia (SA Branch): c/- Mr R Carter
16 Broadmeadow Drive Flagstaff Hill 5159. Ph. (08) 270 2056

Millicent National Trust: 16 Burdon Street Millicent 5280 Ms I Bishop Ph. (087) 33 2321

Millicent Oral History Group: PO Box 22 Millicent 5280. Mrs J Chewings
Ph. (087) 33 2367

Minlaton National Trust: PO Box 138 Minlaton 5575. Mrs D Jolly Ph. (088) 53 4306

Mitcham Historical Society: c/- 1 Torrens Street Mitcham 5062. Ms P Oborn
Ph. (08) 271 5091

Moonta National Trust: 3 Simms Cove Road Moonta 5558. Mr T Evans
Ph. (088) 21 3253, (088) 25 2413 (AH)

Mount Barker National Trust: PO Box 171 Mount Barker 5251. Mrs B Bell
Ph. (08) 391 1670

Mount Gambier Heritage Society: PO Box 252 Mount Gambier 5290. Ms D Wiseman
Ph. (087) 25 6510

Mount Gambier National Trust: PO Box 1002 Mount Gambier 5290. Mrs W Monger
Ph. (087) 25 5284

Mount Horrocks Historical Society: PO Box 26 Watervale 5452. Mrs G Pearce
Ph. (088) 43 0185

Mount Lofty Districts Historical Society: c/- Roger Frisby Stirling District Council
PO Box 21 Stirling 5152. Ms J Ahlberg Ph. (08) 339 3818

Mount Lofty National Trust: PO Box 28 Aldgate 5154. Mr T Dyster
Ph. (08) 391 1985

Murray Bridge & Districts Historical Society Inc.: PO Box 1297 Murray Bridge 5253.
Ph. (085) 32 1199 (W), (085) 32 3396 (H)

Museums Australia (SA): c/- Migration Museum 82 Kintore Avenue Adelaide 5000.
Ms K Walsh Ph. (08) 207 7573(W)

Naracoorte National Trust: PO Box 931 Naracoorte 5271. Mrs R Dennis
Ph. (087) 62 3076

National Trust of South Australia: 452 Pulteney Street Adelaide 5000. Ms P Menses
Ph. (08) 223 1655

Naval Historical Society of Australia (SA Chapter): c/- Mr V Pylypenko
24 Idlewild Avenue Aberfoyle Park 5159.

Noarlunga National Trust: c/- 11 Leitch Avenue Port Noarlunga 5167. Mrs V Catterall
Ph. (08) 384 0655, (08) 384 7918 (AH)

Northern Automotive Restoration Club (SA) Inc: c/- Mrs A Hunt 21 Cockburn Road Jamestown 5491. Ph. (086) 64 1590

Northern Yorke Peninsula Rail Preservation Society: c/- Mr P Thomas PO Box 302 Kadina 5554. Paul Thomas (088) 23 3111

Old Government House – see Friends

Oral History Association of Australia (SA Branch): c/- Secretary 122 Kintore Avenue Adelaide 5000. Ms B Robertson Ph. (08) 207 7349 (W), (08) 278 4045 (H)

Orroroo Historical Society: c/- Ms S Shephard Orroroo 5431.

Overland Corner National Trust: PO Box 656 Barmera 5345.

Peake – see Coomandook

Penola History Society: c/- Ms M Muller Penola RSD 5277. Ph. (087) 37 2382 (W), (087) 37 2262 (H)

Penola National Trust: PO Box 261 Penola 5277. Mr G Adam Ph. (087) 37 2250

Pichi Richi Railway Preservation Society Inc.: Quorn Station Railway Terrace Quorn 5433. Mrs S Gray Ph. (08) 264 7439

Pinnaroo Historical Society: c/- Mr W Wurfel PO Box 22 Pinnaroo 5304. Ph. (085) 77 8115

Pioneers Association of South Australia: 13 Leigh Street Adelaide 5000. Mr P Cudmore Ph. (08) 231 5055

Police – see South Australian

Port Adelaide Historical Society Inc: PO Box 254 Port Adelaide 5015. Mr L Shields Ph. (08) 345 5930

Port Augusta Family History Group: c/- L Fennell 1 Scharenberg Court Port Augusta 5700. Ph. (086) 42 5305

Port Broughton Historical Committee: c/- Mrs J Walton 41 Kerley Street Port Broughton 5522. Ph. (086) 35 2535

Port Dock Station Railway Museum: PO Box 624 Port Adelaide 5015. Mr R Thompson Ph. (08) 341 1654

Port Elliot National Trust: PO Box 260 Port Elliot 5212. Mrs R Mitchell Ph. (085) 54 2180

Port Lincoln National Trust: c/- 42 Lincoln Highway Port Lincoln 5606. Mr E O'Connor Ph. (086) 82 2173

Port Lincoln Pioneers & Descendants Club: c/- Mrs Miller 42 Dublin Street Port Lincoln 5606.

Port of Goolwa & Inland Rivers Historical Society: c/- Signal Point PO Box 1988 Goolwa 5214. Ph. (085) 55 3488

Port Pirie Diocesan History Society: c/- Fr F Cresp PO Box 90 Snowtown 5520. Ph. (088) 65 2264

Port Pirie Family History Group: PO Box 585 Port Pirie 5540.

Port Pirie National Trust: c/- 184 Balmoral Road Port Pirie 5540. Mr I Wood Ph. (086) 32 1080, (086) 32 2272 (AH)

Postal Stationery and Postal History Society of Australia Inc: GPO Box 4 Adelaide 5001.

Professional Historians – see Association of

Queen Adelaide Society: GPO Box 908 Adelaide 5001. Mrs M Hignett Ph. (08) 276 7706

Quorn Local History Group: c/- B Stephenson Joyce Street Quorn 5433. Ph. (086) 48 6094

Railway – see Australian, Ghan, Northern Yorke, Pichi Richi, Port Dock, Steamtown

Renmark National Trust: c/- 56 James Avenue Renmark 5341. Mrs E Loveday
    Ph. (085) 86 6091
Renmark, Paringa & Cal-Lal Historical Preservation Society: c/- Mr P Leuders
    PO Box 155 Renmark 5341.
Riverland Family History Group: PO Box 234 Loxton 5333. Ph. (085) 82 1796
Robe National Trust: PO Box 324 Robe 5276. Mrs D Shaw Ph. (087) 68 2419
Robe Oral History Group: c/- Mrs S Ling Mount Benson Roadside Kingston 5275.
Rocky River Historic & Art Society Inc.: PO Box 18 Laura 5480. R D Biles
    Ph. (086) 62 2171 (W), (086) 63 2582 (H)
Royal Adelaide Hospital Heritage and History Committee: c/- Mr W E J Ricketts RAH
    North Terrace Adelaide 5000. Ph. (08) 224 5303 (W), (08) 264 1132 (H)
Royal Geographical Society of Australasia (SA Branch): c/- State Library of SA
    North Terrace Adelaide 5000. Ms V Sitters Ph. (08) 207 7266
Saddleworth & District Historical Society: c/- Mrs E Williams 12 Charles Street
    Saddleworth 5413.
Sagasco – see South Australian
Salisbury & District Historical Society: PO Box 838 Salisbury 5108. Mr V Gadsby
    Ph. (08) 258 4792
Science – see History
Society for the Study of Labour History (Adelaide Branch): Mr F Hauben
    37 Thomas Street Croydon 5008.
Society for Underwater Historical Research: PO Box 181 North Adelaide 5006.
    Mr P Christopher Ph. (08) 205 3224 (W)
South Australia – see Historical Society of
South Australian Dental Service Heritage and History Committee: c/- Mr W Ricketts
    Adelaide Dental Hospital Frome Road Adelaide 5000. Ph. (08) 223 9211 (W),
    (08) 264 1132 (H)
South Australian Gas Company Historical Group: c/- Mr G Maloney GPO Box 1199
    Adelaide 5001. Ph. (08) 217 2708 (W), (08) 373 0804 (H)
South Australian Genealogy & Heraldry Society Inc.: GPO Box 592 Adelaide 5001.
    Mr R Blair Ph. (08) 272 4222
South Australian Historical Aviation Museum: GPO Box 987 Adelaide 5001.
    Ph. (08) 213 0193 (W), (08) 278 5328 (H)
South Australian Horse Driving Society: c/- Mr J Bull 249 Victoria Road Largs Bay 5016.
    Ph. (08) 497 343
South Australian Light Horse Historical Association: c/- Mrs J Hopkins 4 Lauder Avenue
    Sefton Park 5083. Ph. (08) 269 4644
South Australian Medical Heritage Society: 50 Penno Parade North Belair 5052.
South Australian Metropolitan Fire Service Historical Society: c/- Station Officer M
    Bryant SA Fire Brigade Headquarters Wakefield Street Adelaide 5000.
South Australian Museum of Firefighting Inc: PO Box 105 Christies Beach 5165.
South Australian Police Historical Society: 30 Flinders Street Adelaide 5000. Sgt R Clyne
    Ph. (08) 274 8597 (W), (08) 271 0386 (H)
South Australian Women's History Task Force: c/- Dr S Magarey Research Centre for
    Women's Studies University of Adelaide Adelaide 5000.
South East Family History Group: PO Box 758 Millicent 5280. Mrs R J McCourt
    Ph. (087) 35 2039 (W), (087) 35 2032 (H)

Southern Eyre Peninsula Family History Group: PO Box 1683 Port Lincoln 5606.
    Kevin Harvey (086) 82 1023
Spalding History & Archives Group: c/- Mrs J Trengove Spalding 5454.
Sporting Car Club of South Australia Inc.: 51 King William Road Unley 5061.
    Ph. (08) 373 4899 Fax (08) 373 4703
St John's Ambulance Historical Society: c/- Mr R Schilling PO Box 23 Eastwood 5063.
State Aboriginal Heritage Committee: Culture & Site Services Section State Dept of
    Aboriginal Affairs GPO Box 1563 Adelaide 5001. Mr P Fitzpatrick Ph. (08) 226 8900
Steamtown Peterborough Railway Preservation Society: PO Box 133 Peterborough 5422.
    Mr M Koch Ph. (086) 51 2154
Stirling – see Mount Lofty
Strathalbyn National Trust: c/- 25 Manse Road Strathalbyn 5255. Mrs B Muller
    Ph. (085) 36 2478
Streaky Bay National Trust: c/- 47 Alfred Terrace Streaky Bay 5680. Mrs M Kelsh OAM
    Ph. (086) 261 040
Tatiara National Trust: 81 McLeod Street Bordertown 5268. Mr J Guy
    Ph. (087) 52 1717
Tea Tree Gully National Trust: c/- Ms M Gourley 35 Zenobia Crescent Modbury North 5090.
    Ph. (08) 264 1644
Technology – see History
Terowie Citizen's Association Inc.: c/- Ms M Gray PO Box 12 Terowie 5421.
    Ph. (086) 59 1087 (W), (086) 59 1105 (H)
Terowie National Trust: Post Office Terowie 5421. Mrs M Gray Ph. (086) 59 1105
Theatre History – see Australian
Thebarton Historical Society: c/- Mr K Kaeding 2/438 Grange Road Fulham Gardens 5024.
Tintinara Historical Society: c/- Mrs D Bower PO Box 583 Tintinara 5266.
Torrens Valley & District Historical Society: c/- Mrs D Dowsett Gumeracha 5233.
    Ph. (08) 389 1183 (W), (08) 389 1248 (H)
Trams – see Australian
Tumby Bay National Trust: c/- 9 Tennant Street Tumby Bay 5605. Mrs A J Morris
    Ph. (086) 88 2574
Underwater – see Society
Uniting Church – see Historical Society
Unley National Trust: c/- Mr J McInnes 224 Wattle Street Malvern 5061. John McInnes
    Ph. (08) 226 6838
Vale Park Restorers Club: c/- Allan Carter 3 Harris Road Vale Park 5081.
    Ph. (08) 212 2800 (W); (08) 344 3859 (H)
Victor Harbor National Trust: PO Box 37 Victor Harbor 5211. Mrs B Parsons
    Ph. (085) 52 3323
Victoriana Society of South Australia: c/- Mrs A Collins 137 Coromandel Parade
    Coromandel Valley 5051. Ph. (08) 213 1277 (W), (08) 278 2736 (H)
Waikerie District Historical Society: PO Box 334 Ramco 5322. Mrs M Borroughs
    Ph. (085) 41 2949
Waikerie National Trust: c/- 4 Lawrie Terrace Waikerie 5330. Mrs L Trezise
    Ph. (085) 41 2313
Wallaroo National Trust: PO Box 122 Wallaroo 5556. Mr I Aird Ph. (088) 21 1182,
    (088) 23 2823 (AH)

West Beach Aviation Group: 3 Hallam Street Myrtle Bank 5064. Ph. (08) 338 1205
West Torrens Historical Society: PO Box 43 Cowandilla 5033. Ms M Marles
   Ph. (08) 293 1024
Whyalla National Trust: PO Box 289 Whyalla 5600. Mr B Barber Ph. (086) 45 2437
Williamstown & District Historical Society: c/- Mr T Clemow 34 Wild Street
   Williamstown 5351. Ph. (08) 213 0294 (W), (085) 246 065 (H)
Willunga National Trust: PO Box 429 Willunga 5172. Mrs J Taylor Ph. (085) 56 5114
Women – see South Australian
Woodchester Historical Society: c/- Mr E Cross 5 Adam Street Strathalbyn 5255.
   Mr E Cross Ph. (085) 362 483
Woodville – see Historical Society of
Wudinna & Le Hunte Districts Historical Society: c/- Mrs E G Franklin Yaninee 5653.
   Ph. (086) 80 4019
Yacka Historical Group: c/- Mrs A Tilbrook PO Yacka 5470.
Yankalilla & District Historical Society: c/- Mrs A Johnston PO Box 421 Yankalilla 5203.
Yorke Peninsula Family History Group: PO Box 260 Kadina 5554. Ph. (088) 21 2704
Yorketown Historical Society: c/- Mr H Twartz PO Box 61 Yorketown 5576.
   Ph. (088) 52 1026

SOUTH AUSTRALIAN BIRTHS, DEATHS AND MARRIAGES DISTRICT REGISTERS

A second set of birth, death and marriage registers was maintained for varying dates by district registry offices in South Australia. The number and boundaries of these districts were redefined from time to time. Following the closure of the district registry offices, the South Australian Births, Deaths and Marriages Principal Registry Office, in conjunction with State Records, decided to lodge the district records in local public libraries in the former registration districts. **There is considerable local variation in available material, but, in general, surviving material within the following date ranges has been transferred:**

Births	**1842-1906**
Marriages	**1842-1916**
Deaths	**1842-1967**

The bulk of the entries in the district registers duplicate those held in the general registers at the Births, Deaths and Marriages Principal Registry Office, Adelaide (see page 71).

Each district registrar was required to create an index to registrations in that district and these had their own sets of numbers. The reference numbers on the available indexes to South Australian births, deaths and marriage registers held by the Principle Registry Office will **not** assist in locating records in the district registers.

The South Australian Genealogy and Heraldry Society (see pages 77-78) is working to improve access to information held in the district registers, and is a useful central source of information about them:

- The society has microfiched copies of all the district births, deaths and marriages indexes that have been located to date, and they are available for research at the society library. Holding public libraries may purchase copies of all the indexes, and some may have done so. Copies are **not** held by the State Library. These indexes do **not** include dates.

- Society members have listed libraries with district registers, and their exact holdings. These listings are subject to change as damaged volumes are withdrawn, or as previously missing volumes are found, and the society attempts to keep up to date with these changes.

- Society members are preparing maps showing the boundaries of the districts each time they changed.

- The society has permission to film the district registers for preservation. The society receives a copy as does the library holding the originals. Some records up to 1875 have already been filmed.

The following listing (current to March 1994) of the registration districts (with the commencement year), the public library holding the registers and its holdings is adapted from Maureen M. Leadbeater, 'BDM district records', *South Australian Genealogist,* January 1994, pages 9-13, with permission of the author and with updated information provided by her. An indication of the volumes available or the volumes missing has been included if the full set is not accessible.

If you plan to travel to view district registers, telephone the individual libraries in advance to check hours and availability. Photocopying from district register volumes is not allowed.

1 Adelaide (1842)

Holding library
Unley Civic Centre Library
181 Unley Road
Unley 5061
(08) 372 5117

Available:
Births	1856-1906
Deaths	Mar 1859-1967
Marriages	Mar 1868-1916

Withdrawn damaged:
Births	1879 Jul-Dec, 1880 Jul-Dec, 1881 Jan-Jun, 1882 Jan-Mar, 1883 Jul-Dec, 1887 Apr-Sep, 1895 Jan-Mar, 1896 Oct-Dec
Deaths	1908 Jul-Dec, 1912 Jul-Dec, 1913, 1914 Jan-Jun, 1916 Jan-Jun, 1921 Jan-Jun, 1925 Jan-Jun, 1934 Apr-Jun, 1937 Oct-Dec, 1939 Nov-Dec, 1940 Jan-Sep, 1941 Jan-Jun, 1942 Nov-Dec, 1943 Jan-Feb, 1948-1950, 1951 Jan-Aug, 1952 Jan-Feb
Marriages	1882

2 Hindmarsh (1872)

Not available until July 1995.

3 Port Adelaide (1870)

Holding library
Port Adelaide Public Library
Semaphore Branch
14 Semaphore Road
Semaphore 5019
(08) 49 6888

Available:
Births	1870-1906
Deaths	1870-1915
Marriages	1870-1915

4 Norwood (1882)

Holding library
Campbelltown Public Library
171 Montacute Road
Newton 5074
(08) 366 9299

Missing:
Deaths	1957
Births	1882-Jun 1888, Jan-Jun 1895, Jul 1901-Dec 1903

5 Willunga (1855); Morphett Vale (1856)

Holding library
Noarlunga Library
Ramsay Place
Noarlunga Centre 5168
(08) 384 0655

Available:

Willunga

Births	1857-1874, 1879-1909
Births Index	1869-1874, 1897-1954
Deaths	1856-1874, Nov 1897-1967
Deaths Index	1897-?
Marriages	1879-1899

Morphett Vale

Births	1856-1907
Deaths	1857-1928
Marriages	1871-1907
All indexes	1868-1925

6 Encounter Bay (1855); Yankalilla (1856)

Holding library
Victor Harbor Public Library
10 Coral Street
Victor Harbor 5211
(085) 52 3009

Available:

Encounter Bay

Births	1855-1914
Deaths	1855-1968
Marriages	1854-1901
All indexes	

Yankalilla

Births	1856-1907
Deaths	1856-1928
Marriages	1856-1899
All indexes	

7 Talunga (1856); Highercombe (1856)

Holding library
Tea Tree Gully Library
98 Smart Road
Modbury 5092
(08) 207 8131

Available:

Talunga

Births	1857-1908
Births Index	1866-1974
Deaths	1875-1970
Deaths Index	1909-1971
Marriages	1856-1911
Marriages Index	1856-1976

Highercombe

Births	1875-1909
Deaths	1855 -1856, 1861-1905
Marriages	1855-1905
All indexes	1856-1928

8   Mount Barker (1855); Nairne (1856); Strathalbyn (1856)

Holding library
Mount Barker Community
Library
42 Adelaide Road
Mount Barker 5251
(08) 391 2077

Available:

Mount Barker

Births	1855-1903
Births Index	1875-1940
Deaths	1855-1968
Deaths Index	1893-1990
Marriages	1856-1920
Marriages Index	1894-1972

Nairne

Births	1865-1906
Births Index	1869-1899
Deaths	1856-1868, 1875-1928
Deaths Index	1869-1928
Marriages	1856-1912
Marriages Index	1856-1928

Strathalbyn

Births	1856-1904
Births Index	1865-1907
Deaths	1857-1935
Deaths Index	1857-1935
Marriages	1856-1907
Marriages Index	1881-1893

9   Angaston (1856); Crawford (1856)

Holding library
Barossa Valley Public Library
Murray Street
Nuriootpa 5355
(085) 62 1107

Available:

Angaston

Births	1856-1906
Deaths	1856-1970
Marriages	1856-1906

Crawford

Births	1856-1904
Deaths	1857-1904
Marriages	1875-1904

10 Barossa (1855); Port Gawler (1856); Gawler (1935)

Holding library
Gawler Public Library
Town Hall
89-91 Murray Street
Gawler 5118
(085) 22 1533

Available:
Pt Gawler

Births	1856-1906
Deaths	1856-1925, 1931-1954, 1958-1968
Deaths Index	1886-1912
Marriages	1856-1904
Marriages Index	1886-1912

Barossa

Births	1856-1907
Births Index	1875-1928
Deaths	1856-1930
Deaths Index	1875-1967
Marriages	1856-1912
Marriages Index	1875-1929

11 Gilbert (1856); Upper Wakefield (1867)

Holding agency
Riverton District Council
6 Masters Street
Riverton 5412
(088) 47 2305

Available:
Gilbert

Births	1856-1906
Births Index	1867-1913
Deaths	1856-1970
Deaths Index	1875-1980
Marriages	1856-1917
Marriages Index	1856-1904

Upper Wakefield

Births	1867-1906
Births Index	1867-1928
Deaths	1867-1928
Deaths Index	1867-1928
Marriages	1867-1904
Marriages Index	1905-1928

12 Kapunda (1856)

Holding library
Kapunda Public Library
51 Main Street
Kapunda 5373
(085) 66 2646

Available:

Births	1856-1907
Births Index	1886, 1887, 1895-1912
Deaths	1858-1968
Deaths Index	1886, 1895-1990
Marriages	1856-1912
Marriages Index	1868-1884, 1892

13 Daly (1866)

Holding library
Northern Yorke Peninsula
Public Library
48 Graves Street
Kadina 5554
(088) 21 2704

Available:
Births	1866-1906
Deaths	1866-1916
Marriages	1867-1915

14 Clare (1856)

Holding library
Clare Public Library
33 Old North Road
Clare 5453
(088) 42 3817

15 Pirie (1935)

Holding library
Port Pirie Public Library
Ellen Street
Port Pirie 5540
(086) 32 1649

Available:
Deaths	1935-1970

Not Available:
Births
Marriages

16 'old' Murray (1848) renamed Burra

Holding library
Burra Community Library
7 Bridge Terrace
Burra 5417
(088) 92 2038

Available:
Births	1848-Jun 1904
Births Index	Sep 1848-Aug 1920
Deaths	1848-1953
Deaths Index	1848-1991
Marriages	1851-1919
Marriages Index	1848-1944

17 Frome (1857)

Holding library
Port Augusta Public Library
Civic Centre,
4 Mackay Street
Port Augusta 5700
(086) 41 9149

Available:
Births	1858-Mar 1877, 1879-1905
Births Indexes	all
Deaths	1858-1967
Marriages	1859-1914
Marriages Index	to 1922

Missing:
Deaths Index	1874-1883, 1948-1967

18 Flinders (1842)

Holding library
Port Lincoln Public Library
2 London Street
Port Lincoln 5606
(086) 82 0622

Available:

Births	1875-1907
Births Index	1897-1922
Deaths	1875-1968
Deaths Index	1897-1983
Marriages	1897-1916
Marriages Index	1897-1939

19 Murray (1928)

Holding library
Berri Public Library
Wilson Street
Berri 5343
(085) 82 1922

Available:

Deaths	1929-1967
Deaths Index	1929-1991

20 Wellington (1856); Pinnaroo (1928)

Holding library
Murray Bridge Public Library
Sixth Street
Murray Bridge 5253
(085) 32 1523

Missing:
Wellington

Marriages	1875-1893

21 Robe (1856)

Holding library
Naracoorte Public Library
De Garis Place
Naracoorte 5271
(087) 62 2338

Available:

Births	1859-1906
Deaths	1858-1906, 1923-1969
Marriages	1856-1916

22 Grey (1855)

Holding library
Mount Gambier Public Library
Civic Centre
10 Watson Terrace
Mount Gambier 5290
(087) 24 1727

INDEX

The bibliography *Researching family history*, and individual organisations listed in Part 5
Research agents, societies and district registers are not covered in this index.